FAITH, DOUBT, AND OTHER LINES I'VE CROSSED

FAITH, DOUBT, AND OTHER LINES I'VE CROSSED

WALKING WITH THE UNKNOWN GOD

JAY BAKKER

with ANDY MEISENHEIMER

JERICHO
BOOKS

New York • Boston • Nashville

Scripture quotations are from the New Revised Standard Version Bible, copyright © 1989 by the National Council of the Churches of Christ in the United States of America. Used by permission. All rights reserved.

Jericho Books
Hachette Book Group
237 Park Avenue
New York, NY 10017
www.JerichoBooks.com

Printed in the United States of America

RRD-C

First edition: February 2013
10 9 8 7 6 5 4 3 2 1

Jericho Books is an imprint of FaithWords.
The Jericho Books name and logo are trademarks
of Hachette Book Group, Inc.

The Hachette Speakers Bureau provides a wide range of authors for speaking events. To find out more, go to www.HachetteSpeakersBureau.com or call (866) 376-6591.

The publisher is not responsible for websites (or their content) that are not owned by the publisher.

Library of Congress Cataloging-in-Publication Data
Bakker, Jay.
Faith, doubt, and other lines I've crossed / walking with the unknown God / Jay Bakker with Andy Meisenheimer.—First edition.
    pages cm
Includes bibliographical references.
ISBN 978-0-446-53952-4 (hardcover)—ISBN 978-1-4555-1762-6 (ebook) 1. Faith. 2. Faith—Religious aspects—Christianity.
3. Faith—Biblical teaching. 4. Christian life. I. Meisenheimer, Andy. II. Title.
BV4637.B296 2013
234'.23—dc23
                                                              2012041086

For my sister, Tammy Sue
—J. B.

For Mandy
—A. M.

Contents

FAITH, DOUBT, AND OTHER LINES I'VE CROSSED

Introduction

I will probably be eighty years old and still introduced as Jay Bakker, son of Jim and Tammy Faye. In my first book, *Son of a Preacher Man*, I wrote about PTL, my parents, and what it was like to grow up in the shadow of a scandal. In *One Punk Under God*, a documentary that the Sundance Channel produced about me, you can witness just the beginning of the troubles I had at Revolution, the church I started in Atlanta, as I began to be vocally inclusive of LGBTQ individuals in the church. A couple of years after the documentary aired, I wrote *Fall to Grace*, which reintroduces my story from the beginning all the way through to my church Revolution NYC in Brooklyn.

This book, however, isn't about my story—at least not like that.

Instead, this book is a chronicle of my doubt; my doubt about God, about the Bible, about heaven and hell, about atonement, about love, about grace, about relationships, about society, about church, and about theology. And in the end, I believe I've discovered something deeper and more lasting than the evangelical framework I inherited from my family and my church.

In this way, I'm nobody special. I'm just a person walking with God, a person who has experienced loss and pain and doubt. I'm just a pastor in New York City trying to find his way, fight for the marginalized, and welcome the outcast. Scandal will follow me forever, and scandal has made me famous, but my goal is to make grace famous. Because grace is nothing if not scandalous.

This is what happened to my thinking when I tried to let grace affect every part of my life, even my doubt. That's the story of this book—grace as theology and practice.

Chapter 1

Walking with the Unknown God

Love is the infinite which is given to the finite.

—Paul Tillich, The New Being

1 *God is good, all the time.*
All the time, God is good.
Do you ever stop to consider some of the things people say about God?

How great is our God.

Our songs and prayers, often filled with worn phrases and clichés—do we consider what they sound like to those who are unfamiliar with them?

Ascribe glory to the living God.

Are we thinking about what they really mean? Or do we just assume that if we grew up saying them, if our pastors and leaders say them, they must be meaningful?

Lately I've grown aware of these phrases. I've tried to hear them as if I'd never heard them before. And I've realized that, for me, the questions they bring up are more concerning than the answers they supposedly give. I am beginning to doubt the benefit in our definitive statements about God. The more people say God *is* something, the more I find myself saying God *isn't*.

2 God is *everywhere*, and I don't mean in that mystical, as-close-as-your-very-breath way. There are Gods everywhere you go. I'm capitalizing "God" when I use it this way because no one thinks that their God is just "a" god. This is not everyday idolatry, like "money" or "football." My dad used to preach a sermon that archaeologists would someday say about us, "What beautiful temples you built for your gods!" and they'd be talking about shopping malls and sports stadiums.

I'm not talking about shopping or sports.

This is dead serious, I-think-my-God-is-*the*-God idolatry. This is true idolatry.

There are hundreds of Gods—every nation, religion, denomination, culture, and family has them. And everyone calls their God "God." On street corners and television stations, people try to sell you on their God. They aren't secretive about it. They don't

4

hint. They say outright that "God told me this" and "God doesn't like that" and "That's not of God." And if they are crazy enough, their sayings make it on YouTube and into the hands of bloggers and tweeters with their hashtag battles and flame wars—with little thought about what's actually being said on either side. Everyone's really just saying, "Well, *my* God..."

3 Consider this popular idea: you and another person just happen across each other with what seems like perfect timing, but it's not just a coincidence, right? It's a God thing. A moment that God ordained. This good, important meeting feels like destiny to you. Say you meet some Christian on an airplane who gets you a great deal on insurance. You're thinking, What a God moment!

But what does it mean to someone who isn't familiar with "a God moment"? It sounds like God's in the business of setting up meet-and-greets between wealthy Americans while ignoring the genocide raging in Darfur, the millions around the world living without clean water, the babies dying from malnutrition, and the drunks who get in cars and crash into new parents on their way home from the hospital.

Have we thought about what it says about God that God can arrange "moments" but fails to prevent catastrophe? What kind of God is that?

4 So these are our Gods:

God who wants me to have everything, from the perfect kids to the perfect 401(k) amount when I retire.

God who makes me feel guilty about my running water and functioning electricity and makes me wonder why I'm not feeding children somewhere in a desert.

God who wants me to be a manly man and hunt and fish and look lustfully at my wife.

God who wants me to vote Republican and fight abortion and win wars.

God who wants me to camp out with college students and fight The Man over injustice.

God who is angry and wants me to repent of my filthy sins or be sent to hell.

God who has a spouse in mind for me if only I keep myself a virgin.

God who has a plan for my life and wants me to be—I don't know—driven by purpose.

God who causes natural disasters to warn us of our sin.

Hidden behind all these Gods is, I suspect, a reflection of our own prejudices, our inherent selfishness. When the old, beat-up family van starts in the morning, we say, "Thank you, Jesus!" (because we know we should have had the oil changed weeks ago). But when it breaks down in the middle of the day, we say "Why, God? What am I doing wrong?" (as if we've forgotten about the oil change we should have gotten). As if God is up in the sky looking down and, upon seeing our sin, decides to break down the van, hoping we'll connect the two and shape up and fly right.

One moment, I think that God is blessing me. Look at everything going my way. Next moment, I think that God must be unhappy with me, 'cause look at all the crap happening in my life.

We're convinced that the events of our lives are both our fault and not our fault. We use language that invokes meaning in the smallest of circumstances. "I'm so blessed right now" or "the enemy is really attacking me" or "God must be trying to get my attention." Everything turns out to be a cosmic message to us from God—do this, don't do this, go there, don't go there.

And this self-centered view of God plays itself out in a cosmic way for many evangelicals. God is a loving father who says, "Sure do love you, but if you don't love me in return, I'm afraid I'm going to have to take you out back and beat you to death. For eternity. This is justice. Trust me. Even though I created you good, you screwed it up, and that makes you deserving of my judgment more than being created in my image makes you deserving of my mercy."

5 These Gods are so much like us that I wonder if we may be using them to excuse our own actions. Blaise Pascal wrote that God created us in his own image, and we returned the favor. So if we are angry, we create the angry God. If we are rich, we create the wealthy God. If we are conservative, the conservative God. If we are liberal, the liberal God.

God hates what we hate.

God loves what we love.

And so the same contradictions found in our ideas are found in our God.

The rich God wants you to be rich, but he must have forgotten to tell Jesus, who told the rich to sell all they had and give it to the poor.

The permissive God—you know, who allows things to happen according to his will—doesn't make much sense unless rape is somehow God's will.

The God of war? Well, it's hard to tell his reasons for choosing which wars are just. Why Iraq and not Darfur? Why turn a blind eye to Rwanda? It's funny how this God chooses sides but never seems to tell each side which was chosen.*

The pro-life/pro-death-penalty God is concerned

---

* I was watching this old war movie called *The Longest Day* (Twentieth Century Fox, 1962). First the Americans ask, "Whose side is God really on in this war?" Then an hour later in the movie the Germans ask, "Whose side is God really on?"

about unborn children until that child commits a capital crime. It's all about the timing with this God. You're not saved by works, but works will get you fried.

6 And so we plead with God to find our keys, to be delivered from addiction, to be healed from cancer, and what happens when we get it? What about your brothers and sisters begging and crying out for God to save them? Why would God answer your prayers and not theirs?

Some say it's a mystery.

Some say it's just action and reaction; life isn't fair.

What if the cancer comes back, your keys have to be replaced, or your addictions linger? I've heard people explain how God could be so disappointing by saying—it's our fault. We didn't have enough faith. God must only do things when we believe hard enough. That's why God doesn't act on our behalf.

But tragedy is just that—tragic. And when we search for explanations, we end up not allowing ourselves to ask the questions about God that we want to ask.

Why isn't God showing up?

Why isn't God doing anything?

Where is God?

These are questions that "it's a mystery" and "you

didn't have enough faith" don't answer. And they are questions we must be free to ask.

7 The God I was raised with was very particular about the things you did and did not do. My life was about how to please God, how to get God's approval. So either I was doing and not doing the right things and God was happy, or I was sinning and God was disappointed in me.

God, of course, was always disappointed with me.

This God broke me. Not like you might hear, "I'm broken, a broken vessel, use me Lord," but I was actually *broken*; a mistake, a mess-up, an irregular.

So when I first heard about the God of love, I couldn't believe it. Grace? Love? Mercy? Forgiveness? These didn't make sense. God, as I understood him, wanted me to not look at pornography and not listen to secular music. God wanted me to not steal, to not lie to my parents, to obey my parents even when they were wrong.

But then I was confronted with the idea that God loves me just the way I am, and not the way I should be. That I was accepted, period. Who is this God? I wondered.

I didn't know this God. I knew the disappointed God, the micromanaging-my-behavior God. I didn't know the God of grace.

But I wanted to.

8 I shouldn't have been surprised by the God of love.

Jesus says that the greatest commandment is to love God and love your neighbor as yourself. Of course, his hearers asked, "Who is our neighbor?" perhaps thinking that Jesus would give a nice, manageable boundary like fifty feet, but Jesus says that your enemy is your neighbor. Do good, Jesus says, to those who persecute you.

Jesus tells his disciples on the night he is betrayed that his one command for them is to love each other as he has loved them. And then he gives his life for them. "No one has greater love than this," he says, "than to lay down one's life for one's friends." Love until it kills you because sometimes that's what love does.

I shouldn't have been as surprised as I was by this God of love, but I'd lived too long with other Gods.

9 In the book of Acts, Paul goes to Athens and is distressed by the many idols in the city. He looks around and he sees Gods all over the place.* So Paul meets the Athenians up on the Areopagus (which

---

* Would Paul look at the world today—Christians today—and feel the same distress at our many Gods? Because I wonder what the real difference is between worshipping a goddess of fertility and the God of virginity. Both bless you as long as they are pleased with your behavior or your sacrifice.

the Romans later called Mars Hill) and he tells them, "I see how extremely religious you are in every way. For as I went through the city and looked carefully at the objects of your worship, I found among them an altar with the inscription, 'To an unknown god.' What therefore you worship as unknown, this I proclaim to you."*

This unknown God, Paul says, does not live in shrines made by human hands nor is he served by human hands. God is not gold or silver, stone or image, formed by the art or imagination of any mortal.

He tells them that God, the one who made the world and everything in it, who gives everyone life and breath and all things, is the *unknown* God.

10 Paul writes a passage to the Corinthians you just might have heard before—maybe someone's told you about it. It's pretty groovy. It's 1 Corinthians 13. People read it at weddings. But Paul had no thought of it being applied to weddings. Back then, marriage was about property and ownership and it was nothing like today's exchanging of rings, vows, and proclamations of love. Paul wasn't thinking, you know, one day marriage will be revolutionized and this is going to be the scripture they read 98 percent of the time. He would have copyrighted it if he had known. Imagine the royalty checks right there for the Tarsus family heirs.

---

* Acts 17:22–23.

Instead, Paul is inspired by this command of Jesus to love one another, and he goes on a rant about how useless everything else is without love.

If I speak in the tongues of mortals and of angels, but do not have love, I am a noisy gong or a clanging cymbal. And if I have prophetic powers, and understand all mysteries and all knowledge, and if I have all faith, so as to remove mountains, but do not have love, I am nothing.*

11 Try this sometime—put in "God is love" on Twitter or Facebook and see what happens. *Sure, but that's just one aspect of God's personality.*†

God has many attributes.
God is holy.
God is just.
God is truth, and truth hurts.
God is a God of wrath.
Love is not the only attribute of God.
Love is not God.

I understand it's not easy to think of God as love. It seems impossible to love all people. Some people I have trouble loving. I honestly wish their tongue

---

* 1 Corinthians 13:1–2.

† God has personality? Is God sanguine or phlegmatic? Type A? Eagle, tiger, or rabbit?

would fall out to the glory of God so that they'll stop saying such ridiculous things in the name of Christianity. We all have to work every day to love some people. And sometimes love itself is miserable. You try to love, to never leave, to never forsake, and it all falls apart anyway.

But look what Paul is doing in this passage. It's almost as if he's describing *God*.

Tongues of mortals and angels?

Prophetic power?

All mysteries and knowledge?

Removing mountains?

Giving away all one's possessions and handing over one's body?

He's saying that even with all of the powers of God, without love, it is nothing.

Without *love*, Christ's death on the cross is nothing.

Not "without holiness."

Not "without wrath."

Not "without truth."

Without love.

This isn't a mysterious love that might twist around and become wrath, either. Paul explains it as patient and kind, not rude or boastful or arrogant. It does not insist on its own way, it is not irritable or resentful. *It keeps no record of wrongs.*

I don't see how we can credit God with these attributes of holiness and justice and wrath and vengeance. I am not convinced by those who say we have to accept the tension between love and wrath, grace and holiness; that we have to take this on faith, have it remain a mystery. Because Paul clearly says that while faith and hope remain, the greatest of these is love. Love, Paul says, trumps everything. Without love, everything else is nothing.

12 It's easy to read this scene on the Areopagus as Paul introducing the Athenians to the unknown God so they can now think of this God as *known*, but what if Paul isn't contradicting the *unknown* part? What if Paul is saying that this *unknown* God is the God of all things and cannot be known?

You can't wrap your mind around this God.

You can't get this God under your thumb.

You can't imagine this God on your side.

13 Right before Paul talks about love, he talks about unity.

"If all were a single member, where would the body be? . . . The eye cannot say to the hand, 'I have no need of you,' nor again the head to the feet, 'I have no need for you.' "* Paul says that the weaker members of the body are actually indispensable, that the less honorable are clothed with honor—which is completely backward from what you'd expect. "If

---

* 1 Corinthians 12:19, 21.

one member suffers, all suffer together with it; if one member is honored, all rejoice together with it."*

Once we feel we have figured God out, we start to pull away from others who disagree with our God—who is so much like us. We start to separate, to form different groups around our understanding of God. We stop admitting that we are together, that we are what Paul described as *one body*.

But when we think we know the secret—that we are the ones with the Batphone, so when Gotham's in trouble, they're going to call *us*—we end up being a foot that thinks it's a body and a hand that thinks it's a body. We think we are preserving The Way and The Truth.

But by simply subscribing to one particular idea, we are missing the point.

If we have faith to remove mountains, but have not love—

If we can speak in all tongues, but have not love—

If we give everything away, but have not love—

Somewhere along the way, we got focused on who does what with their genitals and forgot about love.

14 I wonder if it is beside the point to place blame when the keys are missing or found, when the van breaks down or miraculously starts, when someone dies or is healed of cancer.

---

* 1 Corinthians 12:26.

Those things happen. As they happen, I have found that we can discover God by choosing to love others in the midst of it. Instead of looking for the God of punishment or the God of blessing—instead of trying to find God in the circumstances, what if God is found in the love between us?

Theologian Paul Tillich says that love "creates something new out of the destruction caused by death; it bears everything and overcomes everything. It is at work where the power of death is strongest, in war and persecution and homelessness and hunger and physical death itself."

It is love that took Jesus to the cross.

Without love, our circumstances are meaningless.

But when we love, we make our circumstances meaningful.

Love is at work where the power of death is strongest. And so we don't have to invent new Gods. We don't have to mystify God's purposes. Whatever destruction is caused by death, God is for love. God is love.

This God *is* everywhere, in fact, in that mystical as-close-as-your-very-breath kind of way. Paul even quotes Epimenides, a Cretan philosopher, that in God "we live and move and have our being." This God does not live in shrines made by human hands nor is he served by human hands. This God is not gold or silver, stone or image, formed by the art or imagination of any mortal. God is instead everywhere.

So how do we love this God, this unknown, mysterious love, who is everywhere and in whom we live and move and have our being? Saint Augustine asks in his *Confessions*, "What then do I love, when I love my God?" I ask that same question, and the answer I get is: my neighbor, my enemy. No wonder Jesus framed those two commandments as one. When we love others, we are loving God.

Chapter 2

Doubting Faith

Serious doubt is confirmation of faith.

—*Paul Tillich,* Dynamics of Faith

1 Things change.

When I was a kid my sister had a record player—it had these glowing lights that shone all around like a disco ball. She'd listen nonstop to Boy George. Then we moved to cassettes, and you could actually record your own music or capture songs off the radio. Years later, I bought my first CD, *Tougher Than Leather.* That's Run DMC, for you kids. I didn't have a CD player, so I sat for a few years without being able to listen to it. I'd just stare at the cover, knowing that there was good music somewhere inside. After that there was the Discman, where you could listen to a CD in the car, with skip protection and extremely important things like that. Now hundreds of hours of music all fit on my phone.

Things change.

I find as a Christian, though, that I've been conditioned to resist change. Christians, it seems, are extremely slow to respond to change. We don't want to ever have been wrong. We want our theology to be something that has lasted for ages and will last for ages. We want the Bible to be easy to understand and simple to interpret and we want it to hold universal truth for all times and places without anyone needing special training or lenses through which to view it. We want a "firm foundation" that is earthquake-proof.

But if history tells us anything, it's that our faith has been used to justify terrible things. Yet it has also been a force for love and acceptance and equality. It all depends on how you read it, what you expect from it, and how willing you are to embrace change.

2 A blogger once took apart my arguments in my last book line by line, and I was left feeling exactly like what he said I was: biblically illiterate, wrong, a heretic. He used Bible verses and everything.

When I read his blog, I asked myself, Why do I even believe all of this? Why do I persist in preaching or trying to figure out God and Jesus? I'm going to keep getting ripped apart by some guy who's got his own blog.

It's not easy, I guess, being a people-pleasing radical.

I was scheduled to speak the next Sunday at church, and I was also making some appearances that week to promote the book. But all I could think about was this guy tearing my faith to shreds. I should quit this whole thing, I thought, and just fade into the background. Open a record store. Become a VCR repairman. (Ever see those late-night infomercials back in the day? "Go to school to become a VCR repairman!" Bet those guys are kicking themselves right now.)

I'm constantly battling the idea of giving up. It's not necessarily because I'm tired. It has much more to do with the fact that I'm not sure I *believe* anymore. My faith, religion, and beliefs have changed through the years. From my upbringing in the Pentecostal church to now, I have changed a lot. And there's also a lot of things that haven't changed, but that I've finally been able to give words to—things that I've felt deep down for a long time but never been able to process because I was told they were off limits or outside of orthodoxy.

They call this *doubt*. It's the sense that faith is crap, life is meaningless, there is no God, the Bible is a fraud, Jesus was just a charismatic man turned mythological figure if he existed at all, and the best we can do in this life is to ward off death as long as possible.

Doubt. It was a bad word growing up.

3 I googled the word "doubt." Google, the great Bible lexicon and Greek dictionary of our times. The first thing I found was James 1:6–8. James is the best book in the New Testament if you're feeling like getting punched in the face. He's always so encouraging.

> But ask in faith, never doubting, for the one who doubts is like a wave of the sea, driven and tossed by the wind; for the doubter, being double-minded and unstable in every way, must not expect to receive anything from the Lord.

Shit.

After that, everything else Google gave me? Websites with clouds and gold crosses and purplish-red backgrounds all saying that doubt is *bad*, that our faith should be *pure* and *blind* and *childlike*. This didn't help.

I'm wondering if Christianity is true, wondering why I still care, and the solution to my doubt is to just stop doubting and have a pure and blind faith? The answer to doubt is "stop it"?

But doubt isn't the *disease*. It's a *symptom*. If I were wondering if there's any reason to not get completely drunk, it doesn't help to be told I shouldn't drink because drinking is *bad*. I know that for me drinking would be a terrible idea. I also know it dulls the pain for a while.

Then I looked to the gospels—hoping Jesus said

something about doubting. Jesus was a nice guy. I'm positive he'll have some great, Zenlike way of incorporating doubt into faith.

> So Peter got out of the boat, starting walking on the water, and came toward Jesus. But when he noticed the strong wind, he became frightened, and beginning to sink, he cried out, "Lord, save me!" Jesus immediately reached out his hand and caught him, saying to him, "You of little faith, why did you doubt?"*

Peter's walking on water and all of a sudden he looks away from Jesus and begins to sink. And Jesus says, Oh—you doubted. You silly fool. Why did you doubt? Your lack of faith made you sink.

When the disciples have trouble healing people (Matthew 17:14–20), Jesus says it's because of their little faith, then mocks them for not even having faith the size of a mustard seed, which is pretty darn small. In Mark 6, Jesus visits his hometown and is amazed at their unbelief. It even keeps him, Mark says, from being able to do miracles in their midst.

This is starting to look really bad for doubting Jay.

So then I thought I would take a look at the origi-

---

* Matthew 14:29–31.

nal languages. Perhaps Jesus wasn't reacting to doubt as we understand it but to something else.

"Doubt" in the dictionary means to question; to waver; to hesitate.

"Doubt" means in Greek the same thing.

If you do a word study on "hell," you get fascinating information about what Jesus and the biblical writers were actually talking about (we'll do that in a later chapter; it doesn't really line up with our modern concept of hell). But do a word study on "doubt," and they're talking about *doubt*.

Shit yet again.

4   But then I discovered this:

They went to a place called Gethsemane; and he said to his disciples, "Sit here while I pray." He took with him Peter and James and John, and began to be distressed and agitated. And he said to them, "I am deeply grieved, even to death; remain here, and keep awake." And going a little farther, he threw himself on the ground and prayed that, if it were possible, the hour might pass from him. He said, "Abba, Father, for you all things are possible; remove this cup from me, yet, not what I want, but what you want."*

---

*   Mark 14:32–37.

Jesus, who would razz his disciples and his hometown and Peter for their lack of faith, suddenly is under pressure and he hesitates. He wavers.

There's something very human about doubt, and yet maybe something supernatural about it. Something divine. If Jesus is doubting, if Jesus is suffering, then maybe doubt and suffering are holy, sacred.

Because that's not the end of Jesus's doubts. As he hangs on a cross, with the priests and teachers of the law and the men who were hanging with him ridiculing him, he cries out in a loud voice, "My God, my God, why have you forsaken me?"*

This is not just doubt—this is despair.

Jesus questions God's presence with him on the cross. We've covered over this moment in scripture, hoping that it's not true, coming up with complicated theologies to explain how and why God actually did abandon Jesus on the cross. But here Jesus doubts the very existence of God in his moment of greatest suffering.

5 Theologian Paul Tillich says that doubt should not be a threat to the spiritual life. Instead, it is an important element of the spiritual life. We are able to doubt because we are "separated *from,* while participating *in*"† what we doubt. In fact,

---

* Matthew 26:46.

† Paul Tillich, *The Courage to Be* (New Haven, Connecticut: Yale University Press, 2000), 48.

he believes that fanaticism and pharisaism are the symptoms of repressed doubt. This is easy to see in today's evangelical world—often those who preach the hardest against a certain sin or vice are personally struggling with that exact thing. So extreme belief, according to Tillich, is what happens when we repress our unbelief. We believe all the more, hoping that our belief will succeed in suppressing our doubt.

But Tillich writes that "doubt is overcome not by repression but by courage. Courage does not deny that there is doubt, but it takes the doubt into itself as an expression of its own finitude and affirms the content of an ultimate concern. Courage does not need the safety of an unquestionable conviction. It includes the risk without which no creative life is possible."*

These are the words that strengthen me when I am doubting. My doubt is the awareness of not having, of being separated from. My faith is my choice to participate in, despite the risk. My doubt is overcome not by repressing it, but by the courage to embrace it.

In Matthew 5, Jesus has a series of pronouncements about the kingdom of God known as the beatitudes. "Blessed are the poor in spirit, for theirs is the kingdom of heaven. Blessed are those who mourn, for they will be comforted. Blessed are the meek, for they will inherit the earth. Blessed are those who hunger and thirst for righteousness, for they will be filled. Blessed are the merciful, for they will receive

---

* Paul Tillich, *The Dynamics of Faith* (New York: HarperOne, 2001), 117–118.

mercy. Blessed are the pure in heart, for they will see God. Blessed are the peacemakers, for they will be called children of God."*

Jesus makes a list of those who are blessed: poor in spirit, mourners, the hungry for justice, the meek, the merciful. Not the faithful, the rich in spirit, the joyful, the satisfied, the upstanding citizen, and the model Christian. I don't think many of us would be surprised if Jesus had also mentioned the doubter: blessed are those who doubt, for they are filled with faith.

6 My doubt has caused me to grow in faith. Growing up, everything was supposed to make sense. Your faith had to be complete. The Bible was free from error. And faith and the Bible had to be protected from those who would attack it. The antidote to doubt? Believe more. Read the Bible more.

The more I studied the Bible, the more I understood it, the more I examined my faith and the faith of others, the more everything turned gray. That's not what I was promised as a kid. I was told that things would get more black and white, that I'd understand God better and see things more clearly.

Nope.

It just got muddier.

The more you find out, the less you know.

They don't prepare you for this when you're a

---

* Matthew 5:3–9.

Christian kid. Maybe that's why many come back from seminary moaning, "I don't know what I believe anymore!" The only preparation they had for seminary was "I know that I know that I know that I know." When you think you have a handle on God, you start to create a structure around your idea of God, and you start to lose sight of why God matters. God becomes something you have to separate yourself from, to stick in a building, to hide behind a curtain, to preserve, conserve, and curate like a museum piece. And then you worry about whether or not others have the same idea of God as you.

I've always had a problem with a God who needs flesh to be burned or killed. Why would God need this? It must seem like the most insignificant thing to God, killing an animal to make a sacrifice. All of these rules—where to worship, how to worship, how to sacrifice. Why does God care? I also don't understand the God who chooses some people for destruction and some people for glory. That never added up to me. I've heard it said that in order for some people to be chosen for heaven, some must be chosen for destruction.* If this super-great, loving person came to you and said, "Eventually I'm going to torture and kill millions of people, but until then, if you can convert people to my religion, then they'll be saved. But you only have a certain amount of time, and I'm not going to tell you how long." You're going to say, "I've got to stop this!" It's like an action movie:

---

* Romans 9:22–23.

"The building's going to explode!"

"We've got to find the bomb!"

"When's it going to explode?"

"Nobody knows!"

If you really believe in God and hell, you ought to be pleading with Jesus, "This isn't a good idea! What about love? And forgiveness? And mercy? Don't do this! You're a nice guy!"

Doubt allows me to read the Bible differently, to find in it a God who is not vengeful. Doubt allows me to read the Bible through different eyes. And doubt keeps me from thinking I've got a handle on God. Doubt encourages me to keep learning, to keep myself open to being wrong.

7 I know a lot of people who are done with Christianity because of their doubt.

Done with church.

Done with God.

Done with the Bible.

I understand. I don't know if it's how I was raised, or the Holy Spirit, but something pulls me back in. (It *must* be the lavish lifestyle.)

Perhaps it's this: I know that there's good in there somewhere.

I read how Christians, using the scriptures, fought against slavery.

I see how Christians, using the scriptures, are fighting for equal rights.

And that renews my faith.

I've been invited a couple of times to speak at churches in the UFMCC denomination—Universal Fellowship of Metropolitan Community Churches— the first church founded on a positive, affirming ministry to gay, lesbian, bisexual, and transgender persons. They've been around since 1968, longer than me, and for the first thirty years of their existence, over twenty of their churches were set on fire by arsonists and fire-bombers, and many more have been vandalized and threatened. One fire claimed the lives of the pastor, assistant pastor, and almost half the congregation.*

I endure hate from those who think same-sex attraction is a sin and call me a heretic, and from those I am fighting for who say they don't need a straight white male speaking for them. I speak on the issue because scripture makes me think it's what Jesus would do. This is the perfect example of why I do what I do. This is how I answer myself now when I am wondering if faith is worth it.

8 I want to hold on to my views lightly, to keep an open mind, and not feel like I've arrived at the end of theology. I want to put people first and live my life. I'm not out to save anyone from hell or win people to Jesus. I'm just trying to follow Jesus

---

* B. A. Robinson, "Attacks on LGBT churches, and churches sympathetic to LGBT concerns," accessed on September 19, 2012. http://www.religioustol-erance.org/hom_arsn.htm.

myself, and help people find grace and peace and acceptance in their lives.

Doubt keeps me sane. Rather than making me like a wave tossed by the sea, it allows me to go on. It allows me to participate in the grace and love of God even though I feel separated from it so often. I would have quit a long time ago if doubt were the ultimate threat to faith.

I find it divine to doubt. But that doesn't mean doubt is not hard and scary. It can shake your foundations—and that's why we have one another, why we have community. We can go through those days of doubt together. I wouldn't be who I am today if it weren't for the people who have been there with me as I question everything. In fact, some of them make me question everything even more.

For others, it's scary to believe. They need a community that says it's okay to go into this with doubts. You don't have to have it all together to belong. We need both faith and doubt.

We need them both because we're not going to find all the answers. That's why Jesus and the writers of scripture talk about the importance of being in a community, the importance of gathering together— even in twos and threes—because often you just need a person who will listen, someone you can lean on and trust.

Together, we can seek the unknown God. We can read the Bible differently. We can recast eternity and rethink the crucifixion and resurrection. We can walk through tragedy and rediscover grace. We can speak up for the marginalized and welcome the outcast. We can set each other and God free from the church.

Together we can be people of doubt and people of faith.

Chapter 3

Reading the Bible Differently

It is time to stop pretending that, read uncritically and out of context, the Bible will set anyone free.

—*Jennifer Wright Knust,* Unprotected Texts

A friend of mine told his grandmother about the classes he was going to be taking that year at his university. Immediately after mentioning his philosophy class, she exclaimed, "Oh, well. We'll be doubling our prayers for you, then."

I've heard this kind of thing before: Don't read them books, they'll chase Jesus away! We all know there's only one book you need to be reading: *the Bible,* which can be understood by anyone without any outside help, contextual understanding, or commentaries.

Translation from the original languages might help—but no more than that!

Perhaps that's what you grew up with too, this insistence that the Bible is all you need to understand the Bible. In fact, some preachers even encourage people *not* to study the Bible. "You can find a Christian on the run when they start doing word studies,"[*] one is on record as saying. Meaning, once Christians start looking at the *original languages* the Bible was written in—and, we assume, looking into the culture the Bible was written in and the original audience the Bible was written for—they've lost their way.

Author Timothy Beal writes about what he calls the "iconic" cultural understanding of the Bible: it is authoritative, unified, practical, accessible, comprehensive, and exclusive.[†] These are the things we expect from the Bible. This understanding is what I inherited from my parents and teachers. They promised each of these things, if only I would study the Bible more. But, Beal writes, just as Aaron fashioned a golden calf for the Israelites in the desert, the modern church invented this iconic understanding.

The idea of the Bible as a divine guidebook, a map for getting through the terra incognita of life, is our golden calf. It's a substitute for the

---

[*] Mars Hill Church, "Jesus Sweats Blood," accessed on September 19, 2012 http://marshill.com/media/luke/jesus-sweats-blood/ajax_transcript?lang=en.

[†] Timothy Beal, *The Rise and Fall of the Bible* (New York: Houghton Mifflin Harcourt, 2010), 4.

wilderness wandering that the life of faith necessarily entails... 'Behold your god'; that is, God's
Word made flesh, bound between two covers,
incarnation by publication. No more guessing,
no more wondering. No more wandering.*

When we turn the Bible into an answer book, we
miss out on the real story, the depth of all that the
Bible has to offer. It's a bunch of historical documents
from different sources, and when we try to make it
read like one book, we miss out on the story of a faith
that grows and evolves from Genesis to Revelation.
And if we don't engage that story, we will fail to see
how *our* story is the same story, a story of growth and
evolution and change. The Bible, in all of its messi-
ness, contradictions, and variations, is a story of evolv-
ing faith, and its most important message? Our faith is
supposed to evolve as well.

2 I love the Bible, I love to study the Bible, and
I love the history of the Bible—how we got it,
how it was written, who wrote it, what it meant
to the original audience. I have that in common with
most evangelicals; Bible study is my great pursuit.
I'm a total Bible geek. Figuring out what the Bible is
saying is extremely important to me. As Peter Rollins
likes to say, the problem with evangelicals isn't that

---

* Beal, *The Rise and Fall of the Bible,* 83.

they take the Bible too literally, it's that they aren't taking the Bible literally enough. Because when you take the Bible seriously, this iconic idea falls apart.

Rob Bell shows us in *Love Wins* what the Bible prescribes about salvation. "Is it what you say, or who you are, or what you do, or what you say you're going to do, or who your friends are, or who you're married to, or whether you give birth to children? Or is it what questions you're asked? Or is it a question you ask in return?"* (I really hope it's how many times you come up to the front to the altar and get on your hands and knees, because I must have done that a hundred and fifty times as a kid. I'm saved for sure.) Jennifer Wright Knust writes about the Bible's contradictory views on sexuality in *Unprotected Texts*: "The Bible does not offer a systematic set of teaching nor a single sexual code, but it does reveal sometimes conflicting attempts on the part of people and groups to define sexual morality, and to do so in the name of God."†

And then there are some pretty freaky violent things in the Bible, too. Have you ever read the psalms of vengeance? Psalm 137 says "O daughter of Babylon, you devastator! Happy shall they be who pay you back for what you have done to us! Happy shall they be who take your little ones and dash them against the rock!"‡ Or this prophecy from Hosea:

* Rob Bell, *Love Wins* (New York: HarperOne, 2011), 16–17.

† Jennifer Wright Knust, *Unprotected Texts* (New York: HarperOne, 2011), p. 17.

‡ Psalm 137:8–9.

"Samaria shall bear her guilt, because she has rebelled against her God; they shall fall by the sword, their little ones shall be dashed in pieces, and their pregnant women ripped open."*

Timothy Beal talks about the story of the Bible as "something akin to the science of chaos...emerging in all its wonderful complexity—'coming to life' if you will—in the course of a long and often chaotic process involving multiple, often conflicting interests and influences."†

If you look at the history of how the Bible came about, you can see exactly what he is referring to. For most of the life of the scriptures, the canon has been in flux; there are variant texts and manuscripts all over the place, and the Bible has been interpreted in hundreds of different ways. The more I study the Bible, the less I've found it to be what I was told it would be.

I don't find it to be the last word on any subject.

It does not speak with one voice.

It is not a practical guide for life.

It is not easily understood, comprehensive, or complete.

The Bible isn't the place for answers. If we look to it for answers, we are expecting what it cannot deliver.

In fact, the Bible doesn't always make a lot of sense. You can find passages about those who are saved and those who are damned, and you can find verses that say all are forgiven, all are loved. You can read about

---

* Hosea 13:16.

† Beal, *The Rise and Fall of the Bible,* 28.

the unforgivable sin and also that nothing can separate you from the love of God. Because the Bible is a collection of books, letters, and poems from a variety of genres—you wouldn't put all the books in a library together and expect them to agree. Not even all the books on one subject. There would be massive problems. When you bind sixty-six pieces of literature together with a leather cover and really thin paper★ and try to force intellectual or historical unity on them, you're going to end up with problems.

I used to preach that the Bible had no mistakes. The Bible was inerrant. If a mistake were to be found, the entire Bible would fall apart, like that scene in *The Dark Knight Rises* where the football field crumbles into the earth. Everything would be meaningless if the Bible was just a collection of human writings without a divine author.

I thought inerrancy meant that I would see heaven and hell and sin and holiness more easily. People told me: it's the lamp of my life, my guidebook. If I were to find a contradiction, it would mean that I was not studying it correctly. That's how I got into studying the Bible. I'd find a contradiction and then research its context and meaning, but that would only confirm that it was indeed a contradiction. Then I discovered something else: we've been misunderstanding all sorts of things.

★   Which doesn't burn very well. I learned that as a young man. I won't tell you why, but let's just say I wasn't burning Bibles. Well, just the blank pages, if you know what I mean.

We've assumed that somehow the authors of the Bible had miraculous, unbiased access to history, instead of their own agendas and interpretations. We've assumed that Jesus's words in the Bible are quoted word-for-word, although there were no recording devices. We've assumed that our way of reading the Bible was the only right way of reading it.

I'm getting a little heretical here, I know; questions about the Bible are okay for most Christians up to a point. I've met many who asked the wrong questions at a Bible study and were asked not to return. They're kicked out not because of wrong answers, but because of wrong *questions*. You can ask questions that fit within a certain framework, that make sense through the "lenses" with which we read scripture. But question the reason we use those lenses, those glasses? Attempt to remove the glasses and see scripture differently? That's what gets you kicked out.

Author Richard Holloway says in his book *Doubts and Loves* that "the real battle for Christians today is... the battle for a sensible approach to that ancient library of books we call the Bible. The Bible was written by human beings, with all the longings, prejudices, and illusions that characterise us as a species."*

We need to remember that when we read the Bible, we're reading someone else's mail. Literally. And it wasn't meant for us to read. But it's not like

---

* Richard Holloway, *Doubts and Loves: What Is Left of Christianity* (Edinburgh: Canongate, 2001), chapter 10.

we'd ever form a club because we found a bunch of letters that didn't belong to us and exclude anyone who didn't believe what the letters said, right? That would be weird.

3 The most important question to ask of anything we read in the Bible, after the text has been understood within its cultural context and interpreted correctly—and before we decide its significance—is: Is it good news? You can ask this whether you are disillusioned with faith or hopeful about your faith. Is it really good news?

I once read a theologian—a hard-core, five-point neo-Calvinist, if that means anything to you—who wrote that you aren't a real Christian if you haven't wept over the scriptures, over the fact that God has destined so many people to hell.

Is that good news?

One of the first things you do when you start asking "is this good news?" is look at the verses that have been used to hurt people. Good news isn't news that hurts. It's news that heals. It's news that sounds like this: *Love your neighbor as yourself. The greatest of these is love. God is love.* So when we see parts of the Bible used to hurt people, we have to ask—what is that really about?

When I first started to view scripture through this lens, one of my biggest frustrations was Paul. Paul would say something in one book and then turn around and say something else in another book that would seem to totally contradict it. For instance, with slaves—Paul tells Philemon that his runaway slave should be accepted back as a brother, not a slave.

Then he writes that slaves should obey their masters.

And then he tells *masters* to tell their slaves to obey their masters.[*]

So which is it?

4 The way I was raised, if a book of the Bible says it was written by Paul, it was written by Paul. But when I started to read more and tried to reconcile Paul's different viewpoints, I discovered that the majority of scholars believe that certain books, especially First and Second Timothy and Titus, were most definitely not written by Paul.

But the books themselves say they were written by Paul.

1 Timothy: "Paul, an apostle of Christ Jesus by the command of God our Savior and of Christ Jesus our hope…"[†]

2 Timothy: "Paul, an apostle of Christ Jesus by the will of God, for the sake of the promise of life that is in Christ Jesus…"[‡]

---

[*] Borg and Crossan, *The First Paul* (New York: HarperOne, 2010), 29–47.

[†] 1 Timothy 1:1.

[‡] 2 Timothy 1:1.

Titus: "Paul, a servant of God and an apostle of Jesus Christ, for the sake of the faith of God's elect..."[*]

I take the Bible seriously. If these books contain evidence that they were forged in Paul's name, then I want to read that evidence and understand it as best as I can.

So I did.[†] And the "pastoral epistles," as they are called, reflect a significant shift in vocabulary for "Paul." They reflect second- or third-generation Christian thinking—of course, Paul was dead by this time. They contradict Paul's message of equality. They introduce church hierarchy and politics, something no other epistle even hints at. Some think they represent the "Romanization" of Christianity, where the correct "order" of society is preserved instead of broken down like the authentic Paul advocates.

If we're taking the Bible seriously, and literally, then we have to consider the idea that Paul didn't write these letters, but that someone else—perhaps with some authentic writings of Paul in front of them, perhaps not—wrote them.

What is even more fascinating is that the pastoral epistles were most likely written because people were taking Paul's (and Jesus's) message of equality seriously. Paul says that in Christ "there is no longer Jew or Greek,

---

[*] Titus 1:1.

[†] Percy Neale Harrison's *The Problem of the Pastoral Epistles* (New York: Cornell University Library, 2009), among other resources.

there is no longer slave or free, there is no longer male or female."* This is what people react against. In their book *The First Paul*, Marcus Borg and John Dominic Crossan call the pastoral epistles writer "reactionary Paul" because of his reaction against Paul's radical equality. Suddenly "Paul" is saying that women can't teach, speak, or even talk in the service, but it's through childbirth that they will be saved. Slaves should just obey their masters. Authority should be structured and respected. The beauty is that these forgeries show us that women were preaching. People were living in inclusive communities. Rich and poor and slave and free were categories that were being left behind in Christ.

And it *scared people.*

I used to think I had to reconcile the Paul of Galatians and the Paul of the pastoral epistles. And it just made me hate Paul. Why would he change his mind?

But most likely he didn't.

He probably didn't write the second statements at all.

5 Part of me is happy to discover evidence that these books are likely forgeries. The pastoral epistles have been used to promote patriarchal, masculine Christianity that has treated women as second-class for centuries. We're still fighting it today.

---

* Galatians 3:28.

Women can vote (Christians used to argue that a woman's vote wouldn't change anything because she'd vote the same way as her husband, the head of the household), but they still are paid less and discriminated against, especially in churches.

But even if these books *were* written by Paul, those who interpret them as patriarchal and masculine miss the point. Even if they were authentic, that doesn't mean that we should model our churches after the words of the books. They were written to a culture from almost two thousand years ago in a different area of the world. We live in a very different culture, one that values women, rejects slavery, rejects racism, one that doesn't worship our emperor as the son of God or participate in sexual rituals for our gods or require sexual favors from our slaves or students. So why would we think the truths these books contain are found in imitating their culture? Is the writer of the pastoral epistles promoting a sexist, chauvinistic culture? Or is the writer attempting to discover a way of following Jesus *within* and often *against* that culture?

So it's important to look for the countercultural things that the biblical writers say. The cultural statements we can expect. The countercultural ones point us to a better reality. Paul's teaching was very inclusive.*

---

* 1 Corinthians 14:33–36, which commands women not to speak in church, is widely regarded as a late addition to the letter and not originally Pauline.

Women were ministers, slaves were free, all were one in the body. This idea was radically countercultural. Which means we can't continue to use the Bible to separate ourselves from other people.

6 People say, "I didn't make up the rules!" They say, "God said it, I believe it, and that settles it." They interpret scripture according to their values and beliefs, and if it doesn't make sense to them, they call it a "mystery." "I don't know," these preachers tell us, "but it's right here in the Bible. I'm not going to pretend like I understand, I just dish out the Bible truths; I don't know how they all work. It's all a mystery. I just trust God." But that's a smoke screen. They do think they have it all down, and to insulate themselves from critique, they're saying that it's not their interpretation, it's God's, and therefore any critique is countered by saying that "God's ways are not our ways."

And thus illiterate reading of scripture becomes God's truth.

This argument was used in the mid-1800s to use the Bible to justify slavery. One clergyman even wrote this in his supposedly biblical defense of slavery:

> If it were a matter to be determined by my personal sympathies, tastes, or feelings, I should be as ready as any man to condemn the institution of

slavery; for all my prejudices of education, habit, and social position, stand entirely opposed to it.*

In reply, abolitionist Daniel Goodwin writes,

Do his "sympathies, tastes, and feeling" which lead to the condemnation of slavery, arise from the better—the more benevolent and charitable— or from the worse, the more selfish part of his nature? And if from the former, was Christianity intended to repress or to encourage and cultivate our better and kindlier feeling?...Were the education and habits he refers to derived from Christian or from ungodly associations and influences? And finally...does not his inmost soul, and do not the sole tenor and spirit of the Word of God and the Blessed Gospel of Christ cry out against the institution of Slavery? Shall it be indeed necessary for a "Christian Bishop" to school down his humane instincts and sympathies, in order to bring them to a level with those of Jesus Christ?†

The church argued that no matter how many arguments you could find to support slavery in scripture, they all "vanish away as smoke" before the general theme of the Bible and Jesus's teachings. You couldn't love your

---

* Daniel R. Goodwin, *Southern Slavery in Its Present Aspects: Containing a Reply to a Late Work of the Bishop of Vermont on Slavery* (New York: J. P. Lippincott; Negro Universities, 1864; reprint, 1969), 22.

† Daniel R. Goodwin, *Southern Slavery in Its Present Aspects,* 22.

neighbor as yourself and also own him as property. The Bible is on the side of freedom, not slavery.

"Love your neighbor as yourself" is a statement that I find historically rich. It's a statement that abolitionist Christians upheld as their final standard in opposing slavery. It's a statement that marriage equality supporters hold up as their reason for fighting for LGBTQ rights. It fuels acceptance, empowerment, and love all over the world.

You can't kick someone out of a Bible study if you are loving them as you would yourself.

You can't deny them a voice in the pulpit if you are loving them as yourself.

You can't deny them a vote, the right to marry, or leadership in the church if you are loving them as yourself.

In my study of scripture, I've come to this conclusion: if it doesn't measure up to the standard of "love your neighbor as yourself"—that is, "do unto others as you would have them do unto you"—then I have to question whether or not I'm understanding it correctly. When I read the Bible, I look to that statement as my final judge of authenticity. It is found in the Old Testament law, in the Gospels, and in the Epistles. Knust agrees, writing, "Some kind of larger principle like 'love thy neighbor' is required if an ethical compass is to be extracted from the biblical witness."*

---

* Jennifer Wright Knust, *Unprotected Texts* (New York: HarperOne, 2011), "Introduction."

7 Love is my trump card. The Bible doesn't ever keep me from accepting and loving other people. If scripture starts to guide me or direct me into a place where I'm treating someone as less than human, I'm either misunderstanding it or it's wrong. And I base this understanding from the teachings of Jesus in the Bible. They screw with my head, and that's a great thing.

To me, the Bible gets better. When I read and study, I am able to see that what never added up to me *shouldn't* add up. Where I thought, "How can this be right?" I discover that the scholars I'm reading say it's *not* right. This isn't Paul. This is someone writing in the name of Paul to counteract Paul.

Paul isn't wishy-washy about slaves.

The church is.

The Bible is.

But Paul isn't.

I never wanted there to be forgeries in the Bible. I never wanted the Bible to contradict itself. But there are and it does. And now, instead of justifying the Bible and trying to prove that it is internally consistent, I am able to see what is truly beautiful and supernatural about it: Christ and his infinite love, which passes all understanding. A Christ who says, "I will die for love."

Because in the end, the radical message of Jesus wasn't "make sure your slaves stay in line as unto the Lord." It was "love your neighbor as yourself."

The Bible gets better. When you start to see the Bible as a collection of books and letters written by different authors (some of them who aren't necessarily who they say they are), you discover a collection of writings that is deeper, more complex, and more profound than ever before. The Bible is even better to me now, because it's no longer a house of cards. I don't have to be afraid that the wind is going to blow and knock over the whole thing. The scripture points to Christ on the cross, and that's where I find my faith. Not in a book. In the person of Christ.

Instead of giving me all the answers or explaining every point of doctrine, the Bible gives me a story of people struggling to live out a certain faith in a certain culture. It doesn't hold the key to a preserved, impeccable faith that then leaves me with the task of discovering that particular brand of truth if I just study hard enough. Instead, I look to the Bible as a starting point for dealing with the ultimate questions.

It doesn't answer every question.

It opens up the possibilities.

8 We ought to question everything, especially the assumptions we hold when reading the Bible. Within our church communities, questions should be allowed, even welcomed. The church shouldn't be so afraid of questions that we don't allow people around us to voice them.

In the parable of the sower in Matthew 13:4–9, the

seeds that grow are the ones that find rich soil. They grow roots down deep, and when plants have deep roots, they can withstand the wind. If your understanding of God and the Bible is rich enough to hold on through questions and doubts, you will grow strong. It's those who are unable to take the Bible seriously who find themselves with shallow roots in hard ground. When I opened myself up to a complex and multi-layered faith, I found that my faith got better with time. If I had allowed questions to tear down my faith, I would have been lost. And I would be useless to the world, a world that needs me to voice my own questions and to journey with other people through their own.

Chapter 4

Dying and Rising with Christ

For Resurrection life is not some turning away from the experience of death that we find in the event of Crucifixion but rather describes a way of living in its very midst.

—*Peter Rollins,* Insurrection

1 Growing up, I was constantly told that I had sin in my life. I wasn't good enough. I didn't belong. I was taught you could be *sinless*, and that I could lose my salvation through sinning. The phrase I heard a lot was "keep a short account with God." As long as you hadn't sinned since your last confession to God, you might just make it to heaven when you died.

I don't believe that anymore, but I still see the effects of this theology at work in my life. When people are angry at me, I assume that the relationship is over. It's done. I have to go. The first thing I do in an argument is to abandon the other person—because otherwise I feel like I will be abandoned. I grew up with an angry God, not a God who loved me no matter what, and I now fear conflict with the people I love because I'm afraid I'll lose them. I'm afraid they'll stop loving me.

Today's church is just as afraid of being abandoned by God. Of being so wrong about our theology or beliefs that we'll be sent straight to hell. So we fixate on sin—especially individual sin, which can be easily observed and recorded. We create rules and regulations and accountability groups and satellite campuses and house churches, all designed to keep people in line and to have control over the message.

2 Afraid of God's wrath, we've created an elaborate system to prove to ourselves exactly how far we are from those who deserve hell. In other words, we've made sin our ultimate concern. We've built rules and regulations so we don't go anywhere near sinning. And in doing so, we've recreated the law. Paul writes in Romans that "I would not have known what it is to covet if the law

had not said, 'You shall not covet.' "* This moral code we've adopted sparks the desire to do exactly what it is against. We've given sin its power back, allowing it to destroy families and churches and people because of how we react to it.

When teenagers get a ring on their finger to remind them of the contract they signed to not have sex before marriage, what do you think they are thinking about all the time?

Sex.

All the time.

When people fail or make mistakes, we distance ourselves from them instead of restoring them. We're so reactionary. We don't seek the lost sheep—we thank God that we aren't like them, and we make sure they don't lead any other sheep astray. This is exactly the attitude that Jesus reacted against with the religious leaders of his day.

3 Jesus came to fulfill the law, he says. But what does this actually mean? Some say that to fulfill the law, he took the law to its furthest extreme and showed us that no one could be saved by the law, and then through his death gave us a better way to be saved: through belief in himself. But as we've

---

* Romans 7:7b.

already talked about, what does it actually mean to get "saved"?

What exactly is this way that is so easy?

Does being "saved" mean believing in a certain set of theological ideas?

How does that differ from having a bunch of regulations to follow?

Why would Jesus replace a system of sacrificing animals for forgiveness with a system of praying and repenting in his name for forgiveness?

Why would he replace a system of following Ten Commandments with a system of still following Ten Commandments?

Jesus's version of fulfilling the law, in practice, looked like this: eating with sinners and rebuking the followers of the law.

He ate with the outcast.

Criticized the righteous.

Fulfilled the law by breaking it.

4 In fact, Jesus sinned. I'm serious. To the teachers of the law, eating with sinners was a sin. Talking with a Samaritan woman was a sin. Picking and eating grain on the Sabbath was a sin. To the teachers of the law, Jesus didn't say, "Great job! You got it right. Here I am, and you guys are the faithful who stuck with it." No, he told them that they had missed the point. That their ideas of sin and grace and kingdom were all wrong. He called them vipers and snakes and whitewashed tombs. He said that every convert they made was going to become twice the son of hell that they were.

Jesus never said to the religious leaders, "Hey, great job, but let's change things up a bit." No, he totally reinterpreted the law. He changed our understanding of scripture. He didn't show us a new way to live; he showed us the only way to live. Paul got this. He understood. He was a teacher of the law, a teacher to the nth degree. He was an expert. And he turned around and became a teacher of grace. He stood up to Peter when Peter started to waffle on the law, and fought against circumcision for Gentile converts. He became a new man, a believer in the radical grace of God through Christ.

Jesus and Paul both spoke of the law in the same way. Paul says in Galatians: "For the whole law is summed up in a single commandment, 'You shall love your neighbor as yourself.'"* And Jesus in the gospels says the same thing. *Love* fulfills the law.

5 The outward, obvious sins are easy. You can create a checklist and ask, "Have you had sex outside of marriage?" and mark down yes or no. But what about the more subtle sins? The kind of sin that cripples us? What about the person who is unable to be herself around her family because she's

---

* Galatians 5:14.

worried about conflict? Or the person who can't speak out because he is afraid of what people will say? What about people-pleasing? What about self-talk that controls us and hinders us? Jesus says, "I say to you that if you are angry with a brother or sister, you will be liable to judgment"*—in other words, our thoughts have consequences. Revenge isn't just harmful when you carry it out. Vengeful thoughts eat away at your own soul.

But when we realize that we're accepted, that even those harmful (as Paul Tillich puts it, the "unacceptable") thoughts are accepted by God, we are free from guilt, free to deal with them and turn from them. That's what "repent" means. It's about *changing the situation*. Begging on your knees for forgiveness was never Jesus's point.

6 So then, what's the big deal about the crucifixion? We grew up with this idea called "atonement"—that Jesus died for our sins. He paid the penalty that we deserved and God forgave our sin.

In Matthew 18 we read this story:

> Then Peter came to him and said to him, "Lord, if another member of the church sins against me, how often should I forgive? As many as seven times?"

---

* Matthew 5:22.

Jesus said to him, "Not seven times, but, I tell you, seventy-seven times."*

You may have heard this passage before, and heard it explained that Jesus doesn't mean to count up to seventy-seven times (or seventy times seven, some manuscripts read). He means to never stop forgiving.

I think that's true, but my question is: does God practice what Jesus teaches here?

Sharon Baker, in her book *Razing Hell,* points out that all the atonement theories, from Anselm to Calvin, have one thing in common: "God would not simply wipe our slate clean of sin by forgiving it."†
We believe in a system where God isn't really forgiving anything. If Jesus died to pay for our sins, what is God forgiving? If the sins are paid for, there's nothing to forgive—God has received "payment" or "satisfaction." God isn't forgiving. Baker illustrates it well: "If Eric owes me $100 and I make him pay me back and then say, 'Now, I forgive you your debt,' he'd think I was nuts!" Any payment on Eric's behalf cancels the need for forgiveness. The only way to truly forgive the $100 Eric owes is to just *forget about it.*

Grace, then, being free, requires nothing. It's not just for the people who do the right thing. It's not just for

---

* Matthew 18:21–22.

† Sharon L. Baker, *Razing Hell* (Louisville, KY: Westminster John Knox Press, 2010), 35.

the people who believe the right thing. It's not just for the people who confess or repent or turn.

A God who asks us to love enemies, forgive those who harm us, and pursue reconciliation and restoration instead of retribution cannot also require some sort of "payment" or "satisfaction" or "substitution."

7 When Jesus dies, things happen that are not easy to explain. "At that moment the curtain of the temple was torn in two, from top to bottom. The earth shook, and the rocks were split."* Tombs open, the dead begin to walk again, and it gets pretty wild.

This curtain that hung in the temple in Jerusalem supposedly separated humanity from God. It's doubly holy, and only at a certain time of the year could a priest go through it. They'd tie a rope to the priest's leg because they never knew if the priest would drop dead simply from being that close to God. Indiana Jones type stuff, right? (And if you've never seen *Raiders of the Lost Ark*, put down this book and go watch it. Really. Not really. If you're reading this in the bookstore, buy it first. Then go watch Indiana Jones.) After I first saw the movie where—spoiler alert!—the Angel of Death melts the faces of a crowd of Nazis, I asked my dad if that could happen, and he said that

---

* Matthew 27:51.

all you had to do was touch the thing and your face would melt off.

So Jesus dies and this thick curtain tears in two. And what was inside?

No water-face from *The Abyss.*

No black hole.

No pile of lost socks or keys or glasses.

No wizard, not even a man.

Nothing.

Maybe Jesus came to tell us that this curtain of separation was an illusion. That God was never in there. That the law was fiction. That the God who demanded sacrifice was an idol.

God was not changing things and coming out from behind the curtain.

God was never found behind the curtain.

What if, by his death, Jesus is saying: Now what? If there's no God hiding behind there, are you still going to love your neighbor? If there's no sacrifice to be made, no reason to be holy, no blessing to be found, will you still do good to those who persecute you? Will you still hope through every circumstance? Will you still feed the hungry and give drink to the thirsty?

There's an AA principle that the way to get out of yourself is to help someone else. You might think you're lazy and stupid and nobody likes you. But when you help someone else, you get your mind off of yourself. It's not by reading the Bible a lot or praying a lot; it's through actively loving other people.

A few years ago, I would have read this chapter,

thrown the book across the room, labeled the poor idiot who wrote this chapter a heretic, and preached a sermon about Jesus dying for our sins so (as long as we believed in him) God wouldn't throw us in hell.

But today I wonder if Jesus died for our sins in a completely different way than we think. Maybe it was so we could understand exactly what the kingdom of God is like. Maybe it's not about giving God his pound of flesh so we would be spared hell. Maybe it's about showing us a way of dying to ourselves and rising again.

8 Early in the book of Acts,* we read the story of a devout follower of the law, Saul (spoiler alert: he eventually becomes Paul). To Saul, Christians were making a mockery of his faith, of the covenant that he believed God had made with the Jewish people. He was so righteous that he couldn't actually stone the Christians, but he could approve of their stoning—the phrase "laid their coats at [his] feet"† means that he approved of this death. And then on the way to Damascus, Saul sees a light from heaven flashing all around him and a voice saying, "Saul, Saul, why do you persecute me?"‡ In 1 Corinthians 15:3–11, Paul explains his conversion this way:

---

* Acts is not only my favorite book of the Bible, but also my favorite body spray. I'll give you a moment to let that sink in.

† Acts 7:58.

‡ Acts 9:4.

For I handed on to you as of first importance what I in turn had received: that Christ died for our sins in accordance with the scriptures, and that he was buried, and that he was raised on the third day in accordance with the scriptures, and that he appeared to Cephas, then to the twelve. Then he appeared to more than five hundred brothers and sisters at one time, most of whom are still alive, though some have died. Then he appeared to James, then to all the apostles. Last of all, as to one untimely born, he appeared also to me. For I am the least of the apostles, unfit to be called an apostle, because I persecuted the church of God. But by the grace of God I am what I am, and his grace toward me has not been in vain. On the contrary, I worked harder than any of them—though it was not I, but the grace of God that is with me.

Jesus died and rose again after three days.

Saul died, blinded on the road to Damascus, and rose again.

Perhaps this dying and rising is what atonement is really about.

Chapter 5

Recasting Eternity

Eternal life is thus fundamentally a transformation in the very way that we exist in the present.

—*Peter Rollins,* Insurrection

1 Once I asked a friend of mine who is a pastor and a universalist the same question everyone probably asks him: What about Hitler? No one wants Hitler in heaven. If anyone deserves hell, we all know it's Hitler.

He turned to me and said: "What you're saying God does is a thousand times worse than anything Hitler ever did. Because if it takes accepting Jesus to get into heaven, then God took all the non-Christian Jews who died at Hitler's hand and damned them to hell for their beliefs. You are saying that whatever Hitler did, God is doing to those same people over and over again for eternity. Is that the God you follow?" he asked me.

I had to admit that it wasn't.

Most of us are confused or conflicted about hell. Unfortunately, we've been so trained that "God's ways are higher than our ways" that we don't allow ourselves to question the traditional belief in the violent, eternal cruelty of hell. We assume that somewhere there's a justification for the God who forgives *as long as you believe* and the God who forgives *as long as you confess,* and if you don't believe or confess before your last breath, then you will spend eternity burning alive.

2 I'd be happy to not say anything about hell. During a recent controversy regarding a well-known pastor's book about the afterlife, I didn't have the expected "setting the record straight on hell" sermon. I'm such a relevant preacher, it's shocking that I missed the boat on this one.

The problem is, I don't think much about hell.

Here's why: The Old Testament afterlife is called *Sheol.* The Hebrews thought everyone went there after they died. It used to be translated "hell," so our traditional understanding of hell has been influenced by that mistranslation. In the New Testament, *Hades* is translated "hell," but it's really just the Greek word for *Sheol.* So there goes that hell. They both just mean "the grave." We're left, then, with *Gehenna,* which is Jesus's term for hell—wait, no, it's Jesus's term for the actual physical location called *Gehenna*. Gehenna was a valley where, in Second Chronicles, something happened with children and fire,* and where, in Jesus's day, an unquenchable fire burned garbage from the city.†

So it isn't as easy as the preachers make it sound to figure out what the Bible says about heaven and hell. First we have to discover how much of our cultural understanding of the afterlife is influencing our reading. And then we have to figure out how much of the first century's cultural understanding of the afterlife was influencing their conversations. Jesus tells a parable about one dead guy tormented in Sheol who is able to see and interact with Abraham on the "other side" of Sheol. His story is not about the details of the afterlife; it's a parable meant to teach something completely different. He's just using the popular view of the afterlife as the setting for his story. If Jesus can do this, then perhaps we have to see other statements, especially those about fire and brimstone, if you will, as dependent on cultural understanding as well.

3 First, our concept of hell is inspired more by Dante's *Inferno* than anything else. Dante has the wicked suffering for eternity according

---

* Possibly child sacrifice, but the writer of Chronicles seems pretty clear that it is terrible.

† Thanks to Jason Boyett for succinctly summing these things up in Relevant magazine. http://www.relevantmagazine.com/god/church/features/18239-one-hell-of-a-question.

to their most horrible sin, and in purgatory he has them suffering for a very long time until they eventually get the message. At no point in *The Inferno* does God ever seem to forgive anyone. You pay what you owe.

But "you pay what you owe" has no room for grace. If I give you a free car and then say all you have to do is pay the monthly loan payments, it's not really a free car, is it?

To me, Dante's hell goes hand in hand with the vengeful God. There are plenty of people who believe and worship this God—it's the God who strikes down enemies, the God who comes with a sword at the end of time, as well as the God invoked when influential preachers interpret natural disasters or tragic events as God's righteous hand bringing warning or punishment to the nation.* This is a God who allows—or worse, *causes*—the murder of innocent people as punishment for murdering innocent people (or some lesser crime like marriage equality). I can't believe that a Christian could ever think the God of love would be capable of this.

But if God is capable of sending most of the people who have ever lived to hell simply because of their theological beliefs, then why not?

---

* For instance, John Piper's claim that Jesus brings tornadoes as warning to the nations, or when Jerry Falwell claimed that September 11 happened because of abortionists and gays. Or Pat Robertson's claims about Haiti. The list goes on.

4 If there's a hell, then here's the problem with heaven*: Martin Luther King Jr. said that "for some strange reason, I can never be what I ought to be until you are what you ought to be."[†] If I end up in heaven—not because I was good but because of grace—how am I going to be satisfied knowing that there are people suffering in hell? If I spend my life working to end genocide in Darfur or bringing clean water to Rwanda, how am I going to live in heaven without working to end the suffering in hell? If I live my life trying to love my enemy and pray for those who persecute me, why would that change after I die?

If that's heaven and hell, God's going to have to deal with Bono, who's going to start a nonprofit to raise hell awareness and lobby for God to do something about the situation in hell. I'd be right there with him.

Don't we learn from grace that *none of us deserves it and yet still we receive it?*

Isn't it love that keeps no record of wrongs?

Isn't it mercy that triumphs over judgment?

I had a dream like this once (not the Martin Luther King Jr. kind of "I have a dream," but I *had* a dream). I'm being shown around heaven, and two of my best friends are there. They tell me, "We're leaving."

---

* Other than it being eternal—some people think eternity anywhere will end up being hell simply because it never ends.

† "Dr. Martin Luther King's 1963 WMU Speech Found," accessed on September 19, 2012, http://www.wmich.edu/~ulib/archives/mlk/transcription.html.

"You're leaving?" I say. "What do you mean leaving?"

They list for me the people they know who are in hell, people they love or care about, and they say they just can't be in heaven. "We're going to hell," they say.

But I just have to see my mom, so I stay.

Eventually I find my mom, but it turns out that she's leaving too, because she knows people in hell and she's going to be with them.

And suddenly I realize that everyone is headed out of heaven and to hell to be with their loved ones. No one is sticking around except for this one guy, a famous pastor. He's not leaving, but he's weeping in front of God's throne, bitterly weeping because his sons* are in hell.

Then I woke up.

5 When you think of justice, you probably think of "God is just," which seems to be the counter for "God is love." But if hell is justice, then I go back to what Paul says: not even death will separate us from God's love. Not even, in other words, God's justice will separate us from God's love.

Because I believe this isn't just God's love for the righteous or for the saved. It's for the world.

---

* I remember this pastor saying—in real life, not the dream—that if God had chosen one of his sons to go to hell, that he would have to give God the glory. That's most certainly where this part of the dream came from.

6 It makes sense that if you are overly concerned with the afterlife, you don't have much motivation to help anyone here and now. Why care about social justice? It's going to be a million times worse in hell, right? And so you're just going to try to get people saved.

I understand the whole "get right with God" thing, the "I don't make the rules" attitude, and all that. But to me, that's a horrible God to be following. The God who will gladly torture you forever but who sent Jesus so a few people might be spared.

Not only do people who really believe in hell stop caring about people's needs here, today, but they start to get confused about people overall. God is gracious and loving and forgiving, they think, but also wrathful and vengeful and angry. And so when they look at "sinners" they don't know whether to view them as the poor lost who can be saved or the willful disobedient headed for damnation. And if they let it sink in too long, they realize that God is patiently "holding back his wrath" for a time. So which attribute of God is really going to win in the end? Love? Or wrath?

This is why I think we see Christians hating other people, because eventually, they believe, God's going to hate these people too. God's going to burn them all in hell forever, so what's the harm in giving them a little hell right now?

When Jesus was asked if he wanted to bring down

hellfire,* he said, "You don't know what you're asking." Perhaps when Christians talk about hell today, Jesus's response would be the same.

7 When Jesus talked about weeping and gnashing of teeth, it reminds me of when I hit bottom with drinking. There was weeping and gnashing of teeth. I felt like I was in utter darkness. I felt hopeless. I felt depressed. I felt despair. I felt like I was in hell. Now amplify that ten million times and let's go further into the dark.

The kid who is getting molested.

The wife getting beaten.

The girl sold into sexual slavery.

And we have the audacity to say that real hell is some afterlife destination where you are punished based on your rejection of a theological idea about Jesus?

The hell that exists, I think, is the hell on earth.

The Jesus thing to do is reach out to the molested child, the beaten wife, and the girl being sold and rescue them from hell.

8 We have a problem. Those people out there who do terrible, evil things should *pay*. When the suffering or oppressed person hears "good news"

---

* Luke 9:54.

they aren't expecting to hear "someday you could be in heaven, and so might your abuser/oppressor." They are expecting deliverance *now*. Their minds aren't on eternity. They are experiencing hell now.

Perhaps all this talk of eternity is simply a way of wrapping our minds around the consequences of our actions. For the person who molests a child, that action has consequences that last for eternity; we can't understand how that one evil act affects people for generations to come. In that way, we might speak of an afterlife. And perhaps this is what Jesus meant when he said that whatever you do to the "least of these," you do to him.

But this realm of justice after death often keeps us from dealing with justice here on earth. We invent hell as a way of getting back at the evil things people do, instead of working here and now to eliminate them, to rescue people from hurt and evil. Hell is a way of convincing ourselves that there's nothing we can do about it now. It's our consolation, our justification for sitting back and doing nothing. In the face of meaningless evil, we invent a system of cosmic justice instead of being the instrument of just change in the world.

But if there's no hell, if there's only love and grace, we have to rediscover what justice means. What kind of justice is available for the world under grace? It's not revenge, an eye for an eye. Grace has no room for that. It's definitely not random violence, like the God who warns nations using natural disasters. That's crazy. I want to see people love one another more, and I don't see how we can do that when we view God as the ultimate torturer. When our God is violent, we justify violence.

But Jesus, I believe, shows us a better way.

I've never actually seen anyone struck down by lightning or fire and brimstone. I have never experienced this violent God. But I have experienced love. And love is what I believe can change the world.

9 So let's look to Jesus and his teachings, because there's a lot of vengeful God in the Old Testament. Maybe it's no surprise that this God still has so many followers today, because if you read the law, there's a lot of not loving your neighbor. A lot of killing your neighbor. A lot of God punishing people without warning or grace. The earth swallowing people up. The death penalty for a handful of unlawful crimes. There's people slaughtered by God's hand and slaughtered because God commanded the people to do so.

But let's look at a fascinating moment in the gospel of Luke where Jesus actually reads from the prophets.

When he came to Nazareth, where he had been brought up, he went to the synagogue on the sabbath day, as was his custom. He stood up to read, and the scroll of the prophet Isaiah was given to him. He unrolled the scroll and found the place where it was written: "The Spirit of the Lord is upon me, because he has anointed me to bring good news to the poor. He has sent me to proclaim release to the captives and recovery of sight to the blind, to let the oppressed go free, to proclaim the year of the Lord's favor." And he rolled up the scroll, gave it back to the attendant, and sat down.*

The most interesting thing here isn't what Jesus says; it's what he doesn't say. He doesn't say, "and the day of vengeance of our God," which is the next line of the Isaiah passage.

If Jesus had tried this in today's churches, there'd be an uproar. If he had said, "For God so loved the world that he *gave*," the church would jump up and say, "Finish the verse!" Jesus finishes in the middle of a sentence, rolls up the scroll, and sits down.

In light of the violence of the God of the Old Testament, Jesus, Paul, and James dare to tell us that all of the law and the prophets are summed up in the statement "love your neighbor as yourself."

The Old Testament is filled with God's wrath.

But Jesus sums all of this up in "love God and love your neighbor as yourself."

Obviously there's something going on here. Jesus is reinterpreting the Old Testament. And he's telling us about a God of love. Not a God who sends natu-

---

* Luke 4:16–20.

ral disasters to "warn" or "punish" nations. And not a God who worries about what your theology is or whether or not you believe the right things.

Jesus reveals to us a God interested in reconciliation and restoration *now*.

10

If I believed God was going to damn people to eternal torture, I would be obsessively concerned with people's eternal destiny, especially mine. I would want to guarantee that I was picked. I would cling to my faith so tightly that nothing could ever shake it.

When I finally realized that I couldn't pull my life together, I just assumed that God hated me, and if I was going to have a chance at heaven it would be a deathbed conversion. I was a teenager, constantly drunk, partying and drinking. Since God hated me, I might as well go with it. But that's when the idea of grace finally sunk in. I was forced to accept that God loved me just the same if I was drunk on the corner of the street or if I was sober and preaching the gospel in crusades across the world. That's when I finally got sober. *After* I found out that I was accepted.

When I lived in Atlanta, pastoring Revolution there, I had a friend who would fight with me about grace. He'd tell me that I was being too weak on sin. That God was holy and couldn't stand to be in the presence of sin. I would go out in the middle of the night and drive this friend home from a bar or party where he'd gotten completely wasted. He knew he could call me at any time and I'd be his chauffeur. He kept on fighting me about grace and kept using drugs and alcohol every night.

Later, after I'd moved to New York City and started a church here, he finally got sober. He told me when we caught up with each other years later that it was because of my constant grace toward him—how I would drive him home every time no matter what— that made him realize that I loved and accepted him, drunk or sober. At the time, he just couldn't accept himself, and he couldn't believe that God accepted him. So he kept on getting drunk every night. But then he realized that if I could accept and love him even as a drunk, then God must as well.

11 Instead of worrying about hell, I'd rather worry about the kingdom of God, which in the scriptures is sometimes called the "kingdom of heaven" out of reverence for the word "God." We've mistaken the idea of "kingdom of heaven" for a heavenly, spiritual thing. But the kingdom of God is a here-and-now thing. It happens here on earth and now in our communities.

The kingdom is where people love their neighbors as themselves. They love their enemy. They become great by serving others. And instead of bragging, getting drunk, or losing themselves in rage, they are filled with peace, patience, kindness, goodness, faithfulness, self-control. Paul says that the "works of the flesh are obvious" and then, after listing them, notes that those who do such things will not inherit the kingdom of God. I used to think that meant that they would go to hell. They wouldn't inherit the kingdom because God would be too busy punishing them. But he was really saying that they will not inherit the kingdom *now*. They will not find peace or patience or kindness.

For who finds peace when they are jealous?

Who finds patience when they are angry?

Who finds self-control when they are addicted?

We can see, then, the kingdom of God when we see people who are patient, forgiving, loving, kind, and faithful. And we see people who aren't inheriting the kingdom of God when they practice unkindness, unforgiveness and hate.

12 If I was saved from something, I was saved from myself. We all have obsessions; we have dark places and secret desires. That's hell. And when we give in to those things—and they take different forms for different people—we discover hell.

And then there are the things that happen to us that cause us hell. Death, disease, loss, divorce—I've been through them, and the people who got me out of those dark places are the ones who bore the fruit of the kingdom of God: patience, kindness, self-control. They taught me to find joy even in my sorrow. To be patient with my grief.

And so I hope for life after death, but I believe in life before death.*

13 But if there is an afterlife, perhaps it will be one of healing. When someone forgives someone here on earth, they are choosing to see past the hurt and the pain and extend grace to that person. Perhaps in the afterlife, we won't recognize people. Perhaps that is the outworking of grace. We must remember that everyone has a story. The victimizer was almost always once a victim. It's scary to judge when exactly the shift takes place, when the victim's past no longer matters, and they become fully responsible for their actions. God's love can heal the wounds that caused the victim to become the victimizer, and they are freed from the psychological trauma of their past. Love is what makes justice just.

14 So the good news for the person in an abusive situation isn't that Jesus died for her sins. It's that she doesn't have to go through this situation. She doesn't have to accept it. That she's actually deserving of love and grace and acceptance, not abuse. If I were I meet this person, I wouldn't

---

* This is stolen from Peter Rollins. Who knows if it's his or someone else's. I think it's the rule of three: first time you give credit, second time "I heard it somewhere," and third time it's "I was thinking about it." Preacher's rule. Third time it's yours.

worry about "her eternal destiny" like I might have in the past, because that seems to make less of what she's going through now. Instead, I would say, "Let's get you out of this situation. You don't have to be afraid anymore. You don't have to put up with this." And to those wondering where Jesus comes into this Gospel, it's Jesus who taught me this. Jesus taught me to value those whom society values least.

This is also true if this person were abusing herself, with drugs or sex or alcohol or the need for people's approval. The good news is the same: You are accepted. You don't need to do these things to yourself. I love and accept you, and God loves and accepts you.

The gospel for the abuser, too, is that he doesn't have to do this. The good news is not that Jesus died for his sins so he can go to heaven, but that limitless love and grace abound for him. He can find peace. There is space for him to figure out why he is compelled to abuse others, so he can learn to control himself and he can make amends. He can be shown that the world isn't a place where you have to do those things, but it can be a place of love and grace. The gospel includes me saying, "Call your family. You're not staying at home tonight. We're going to find you another place to stay and a good counselor and get this straightened out."

The gospel here isn't all in their head, all in their beliefs. It takes me stepping out and doing something to help him and help her. I'm there to act on their behalf in love. The good news is that there are people who care about them and love them enough to help them, and I'm one of those people, even if I'm a stranger or a Samaritan.

You aren't beyond the reach of love, here, now, today.

15 Every day, if I give up some of my lusts and wants and needs to actually help someone else, I become a part of something bigger than myself. It's like AA. When I help other people stay sober, it helps me stay sober. In AA, you aren't aiming at sobriety because someone's going to punish you if you take a drink. You're doing it for your own good and the good of people you love.

I know it's a hippy-dippy-sounding gospel. Jesus was a hippy-dippy-sounding guy. The disciples all expected the Messiah to come in and overthrow Rome and start a revolution and make Jerusalem the capital of a Jewish state and free them from political and economic oppression. Jesus came to bring peace, yes—but not the Roman kind of peace. The Romans thought you could bring peace through war, violence, and domination. "We're going to bring peace to you whether you like it or not, dammit!" (When we were on vacation, my mom used to say, "We're all going to have a good time whether you like it or not, dammit!" I grew up thinking "dammit" was just a vacation word.)

Jesus came and said wash your enemy's feet. Walk with them an extra mile. Pray for them. Turn the other cheek. What Jesus said was much more subversive than it sounds to us today, but even then, this wasn't an active, forceful revolution. This was a subversive revolution, like the nonviolent protests of Martin Luther King Jr. and Gandhi.

Paul says to work out your faith with fear and trembling.* But then we have to keep reading. It's not because God is out to get us if we get it wrong. Nor does Paul want to put you on a guilt trip. There's no fear of hell. Paul says to work out your faith with fear and trembling because it is God at work in you.

History teaches us that if there's anything to fear, it's what other people will do to you. For most of history, if you get it wrong, you die. When you take the road less traveled, when you turn the other cheek or say Christ is Lord, not Caesar, then you will face persecution—sometimes from the world powers, as Gandhi did, but sometimes from the religious powers, from the leaders of the church, from your own brothers and sisters.

16 In an interview I once saw, the parent of a serial killer said, "There's nothing I can do about what he's done, but he is still my

---

* Philippians 2:12.

son. I hate what he did, it terrifies me, but he's still my boy."

This is the type of parent I imagine God to be. Not the parent who, as I have heard over and over again from friends and people I meet, turns away from a son or daughter because of their sexual identity. But a God who, even in the face of terrible evil, says, "He's still my boy."

My hope is that we can start to see eternity and the gospel not as an after-death reality, but a here-and-now reality, one that requires us to dig in and discover daily grace for everyone we meet. We can stop viewing God as ruled by wrath, a God ready to make the evil pay, and instead discover limitless grace—now.

Chapter 6

Rediscovering Grace

[Grace is] not cheap. It's free, and as such will always be the banana peel for the orthodox foot and a fairy tale for the grown-up sensibility.

—*Brennan Manning and John Blase,* All Is Grace

1 I read an article recently that talked about how young Christians are "falling into grace" and forgetting about holiness. Since my last book was titled *Fall to Grace*, I had to read this article. The author was shocked to find out that a young woman in college who considered herself a Christian was sleeping with her boyfriend, partying on Friday nights, and dared to come to church on Sunday mornings. This young woman, he writes, was falling into grace. She clearly wasn't concerned about holiness. He also complains that his former classmate, who used to be a stand-up Christian, has gotten divorced and is now living life "just to be happy." Too much grace, he says. Not enough holiness.

Since writing *Fall to Grace* I have discovered two big concerns people have with grace: 1) That you'll stop caring about the poor or the hungry. You'll just sit in the pew on Sunday, go home, and not do anything. Or, 2) If you grew up like I did, grace would give you license to drink, have sex, watch *The Simpsons*, and play Dungeons and Dragons. Grace bothers people. It makes the guy with the veggie-powered bus afraid people will forget to help the poor. It makes the uptight morality police wonder if people will sleep with everyone they can.

Guess what? They're right. You might realize that you are accepted by God just as you are and ignore the poor. Or you may go sleep with everyone you can. But that shouldn't make us back away from the idea of grace. It's freedom that makes it *grace*.

2 If you're not unsettled by grace, you should be. Grace is unsettling. For it to be grace, it has to be *unfair*. It's "wild, and outrageous, and vulgar."*

---

* Robert Farrar Capon, *The Romance of the Word* (Grand Rapids, MI: Wm. B. Eerdmans Publishing Co., 1996), 20.

No one is ever completely happy with grace. Grace makes you uncomfortable. It doesn't make sense, and it never will. There aren't rules; it is what it is.

We cheapen grace when we make it temporary, a ticket to an afterlife; when we say grace gets you into heaven, but holiness is what is required of you now. If grace isn't about "right now," but instead about "in the future," then we are tempted to make it something we can earn in the time between. We might not have earned grace *before* we received it, but we think we have to continually earn it *again* now that it's ours.

We do this because we desperately want to have some control over grace. We want even the smallest ability to claim that we somehow earned this grace, because then we can have some measure of certainty that we've got it. Which in turn allows us to say that other people don't have it.

If we've earned grace, other people can fail to earn it.

They don't measure up.

They're too far gone.

We think that because we *accept* grace, or acknowledge our need for it, we somehow receive it—and then others who don't accept it or understand it don't receive it. But that's not how grace works. It's not a gift we receive. It's a pull on us that we surrender to.

We have nothing to do with it.

In a way, it's like in *Star Wars* (just the original trilogy, of course) where Luke, with the blast helmet on, is trying to swing and block the training sphere's attacks. He can't see. He can't dodge. All he can do is give in to the all-permeating Force. He can't earn it. He can accept that the Force is there and all around him. But it's there even if he refuses to accept it. That's how grace works.

Christians are always looking for someone or something grace can't cover. So we end up putting restrictions on grace. Come on, Jay, you might say, grace is good—*but*. Grace is good—*but* it's not a license to sin.

Remember the free car? "Every month from now on you'll get a bill, and you'll need to pay it, not because you are earning the car, but out of gratitude for getting a free car." That's how it was taught to me as a kid. Come up here and get forgiven! God loves you and requires nothing back from this love other than *everything you have*. It's like a timeshare presentation. You get home and you realize, "Did I just buy a condo in Orlando? All I wanted were free tickets to Disney World!"

To those who say grace has to be limited, that we have to see some people receive the destruction we all deserve so we might understand the nature of grace, I say the opposite. In order for grace to truly be grace, it has to extend to absolutely everyone, no matter what, no questions, no exceptions. Otherwise we think that somehow, by living a moral life or giving to the poor or voting a certain way or dedicating our lives to a certain thing, we've deserved it.

3 Robert Farrar Capon writes that grace is *vulgar.*[*] We might not understand that until we consider that the person we don't want to extend grace to has already had grace extended to them by God. No matter what that person has done to you, they are accepted.

You might be hurt.

Someone you love might be hurt.

This person is at fault.

You don't want to extend grace.

You don't want to accept this person.

But this person is accepted and loved by God. They are still a child of God. You might not be able to extend grace to that person. It might offend you that this person is extended grace. *But grace is theirs too.* And you can't do anything about it.

This is why we are afraid of grace, and should be.

It extends to our enemies.

It extends beyond the gates of hell.

It welcomes in everyone, regardless.

4 Our greatest fear may be that grace reaches even us. Deep down, we are afraid of being accepted. If we see other people being accepted, we have to acknowledge that we, too, are accepted. If we see

---

[*] Capon, *The Romance of the Word,* 20.

other people transformed by grace, we have to admit that we, too, ought to be even more transformed by grace. So we keep it all at arm's length. We forgive and show grace to others just enough to prove that we understand grace.

But we never let it overwhelm us.

Our fear of grace is just like Yoda said: fear leads to anger, anger leads to hate, and hate leads to suffering. Rather than being humbled and baffled by grace, we draw lines around who is in and who is out and pretend we've done something to earn grace. Our fear that we are accepted *no matter what* leads us to restrict grace, to redefine it, as if somehow we could possibly understand or control grace. We allow ourselves to hate those who aren't "in," and we torture ourselves with needing to constantly prove that we ourselves are still a part of the right crowd.

Instead of redefining grace to exclude our enemies, those who have hurt or harmed us in some way, let's get angry at how undiscriminating grace is. It's *unfair* for grace to reach that person. It's vulgar. It's obscene. I don't like knowing that the people I can't stand, the people who speak hate against women, against people of other races, against lesbians and gays, against anyone—those haters are still covered by grace.

They are accepted.

They are loved by God.

I don't like that at all. But that doesn't mean I can limit grace to keep them out. I just have to deal with it, work through it, and maybe be able to show them grace as well.

5 When we're able to tap into self-acceptance— the acceptance of the "unacceptable" into our lives—we begin to be changed. When we see and accept the unacceptable in our own lives, we recognize the unacceptable in other people's lives and yet accept those people anyway. Then we are truly able to help others, to lead them to grace, to help them discover transformation.

That any of us act like moral giants is pretty insane. We all add to suffering, and we ignore it. We know that our chocolate is picked by child laborers, diamonds are mined for slave wages, iPhones are assembled in inhuman working conditions. We can ignore all that, but we freak out when someone sleeps with their secretary. Everyone in church is freaking out, yet they wear diamonds. They eat chocolate. They drink coffee, eat bananas, and run their whole lives from their iPhones, just like I do. These sins aren't as obvious as sleeping with your secretary. But they're real sins, and they probably have a more dire effect on humanity than the sins we gasp at. And they're the ones we all commit.

6 People will live untransformed by grace. Some will use it as an excuse to be uncaring. Others will use it as a license to sin.

But none of them will ever be transformed through *legalism*. They will never be transformed by accusations that they are relying too much on grace, not enough on holiness. When they are transformed, they will be transformed only by grace.

This is a scary, terrible risk, but it's the one to which Jesus calls us.

Grace is sufficient for those of us who might be living untransformed. We are still accepted, still welcomed by God. The power and risk of grace is that it gives us absolute freedom to be transformed by it. Grace is given to us freely. We have it.

We accept it or we don't. But we still have it.

We receive it or we don't. But it is still freely ours.

We are transformed by it or not. If we are, it's the most transformative power we'll ever experience. I want to put an asterisk or something after that statement so everyone is aware of the danger of it. It's that powerful, that volatile.

This is why I'm amazed by it and perplexed by it, and why I've done nothing but talk about it since I realized what it was and got a glimpse of what it could do in my life.

7 Everyone's got villains. Being open-minded and liberal just gives you a new set of villains to hate. Instead of hating those destroying America or attacking your faith, we find ourselves railing against those who think we're destroying America or hating those who believe they have to defend an outdated faith. We hate the haters. But Pat Robertson and Tony Perkins and Mark Driscoll and Fred Phelps deserve grace too. They have kids, spouses, grandkids. They have family, just like I do.

I don't really want to say or write that; I don't want to preach this side of grace because I don't want to extend grace to those people. I want them stopped. Shut down. Silenced.

But if I am accepted, everyone is accepted.

Grace covers me, and grace covers the worst, most vile person I can imagine.

I don't have to accept someone's hurt or hate. I can confront that behavior. But I can't deny that person is covered by grace. Again, Paul Tillich wrote that in order to understand grace, we have to accept the unacceptable in ourselves. But if you want grace to really transform your life, if you want to truly understand and accept the unacceptable in yourself, you have to accept the unacceptable in others.

8 And here might be grace's greatest power: the moment when you can look at someone and say, "You are not my enemy. Your ideas might be my enemy; your message might be my enemy. But *you* are not my enemy. You are a victim of misinformation. That is my enemy: misinformation."

Martin Luther King Jr. said that racism is a misunderstanding. If that's true, heterosexism is a misunderstanding. Hate is a misunderstanding. Grace, then, is realizing that others—the ones we hate, the ones who hurt us or hurt the ones we love—are victims themselves. They are victims of misinformation.

This is how I understand grace toward my enemies. It is not those who practice racism who are my enemies, but racism itself. It is not those who practice homophobia who are my enemies, but homophobia itself. It is not those who preach a sexist, racist, homophobic God who are my enemies, but sexism and racism and homophobia.

9 "Grace is not cheap. It's free, and as such will always be a banana peel to the orthodox foot and a fairy tale for the grown-up sensibility." There's always going to be that orthodox part of us that slips on grace. There's always that grown-up part of us that is going to think grace is too good to be true. Everything inside me tells me that the law makes sense and the law is good and people need rules. We don't react well to the idea that the murderer or the terrorist or the abuser or the bully are covered by grace, that they can be transformed as easily as we can be. Grace cannot be that easy, that simple, that widespread, and that *unjust*.

When we really understand it, we will always find grace offensive. And that's exactly the way it should be. If we start to feel comfortable with grace, then we've lost what it really means.

Chapter 7

Speaking Up for the Marginalized

There is no longer Jew or Greek, there is no longer slave or free, there is no longer male or female.

—Galatians 3:28

1 I married a couple in New York right under the huge Rockefeller Center Christmas tree. It wasn't a huge wedding; there wasn't much of a mob. We had to hurry because we hadn't double-checked to make sure that we could use that space for a wedding. It was quick, but it was fun and beautiful and exciting to do. The couple wasn't from New York; they'd just stopped in to be married. They were two young kids in love and excited to declare their love for each other in a state that recognized their right to be married. Because in the state they called home, they weren't allowed to be married. It was against the law for two women to marry.

But not in New York.

This was 2012.

In 1883, forty states had laws against another type of marriage—interracial marriage. Perhaps you think these laws were to prevent white people from marrying black, but in many states the laws listed several different "races" that white people were not allowed to marry. You could be fined what today would be *millions* of dollars for breaking this law. One couple was sentenced to two years' prison time.

It wasn't until 1948 that the first state repealed its law. And it took nineteen years for the Supreme Court to decide that all interracial marriage bans were unconstitutional. That's 1967 before a non-white person could marry a white person in every state. Not even fifty years ago. If your parents were married before 1967, they are most likely not an interracial couple *by law*.

It took thirty-three more years after the Supreme Court's ruling for Bob Jones University (a Christian college) to drop its ban on interracial dating—a ban that it defended as *biblical* (on Easter 1960, Bob Jones Sr. preached his "most important sermon," one where he argued that segregation was preserving God's plan for the different races according to the

Bible*). But they suddenly dropped their ban—most likely because it was becoming a political issue for President Bush.

2 One hundred years ago, if you were a woman, you weren't considered capable to judge matters of government. You did not get to vote. At the time, many Christians justified this, reasoning that a woman's husband already voted for her. That's right. God decided that a man would be the head of his household, and so a woman didn't need to vote because she would vote the same way as her husband. And the church is still dealing with equality for women. A recent column in the *Washington Post* declared that bias in our churches is the final frontier for feminism.[†]

The church historically has lagged behind government when it comes to these issues of civil liberties—first, women as individuals, then issues of race and segregation—supporting its discrimination with scripture. We are again on the edge of a civil liberties issue,

---

[*] "God is the author of segregation. God is the author of Jewish separation and Gentile separation and Japanese separation. God made of one blood all nations, but He also drew the boundary lines between races." "Is Segregation Scriptural?" by Bob Jones Sr. 1960, accessed on September 19, 2012, http://www.drslewis. org/camille/2011/05/is-segregation-scriptural-by-bob-jones-sr-1960/.

[†] Lisa Miller, "Feminism's Final Frontier? Religion," *Washington Post,* March 8, 2012. http://www.washingtonpost.com/national/on-faith/churches-and-politicians-take-note-disrespect-women-and-they-will-leave/2012/03/07/gIQA9SwJzR_story.html; accessed on September 21, 2012.

ignoring the pattern of our history, using the same fearful tactics.

Instead of leading the charge, fighting for the rights of the oppressed and marginalized, the church might again be the final frontier of discrimination. We're hunkered down and defending outdated cultural values. Every week, there's another Christian in the news talking about what the Bible supposedly says about homosexuality* and claiming that God is on their side—often without any sort of reference to the scripture or Jesus, and almost never with a critical engagement of those texts.

Part of the problem is that people forget what a "right" is. When I talk about supporting equal rights for LGBTQ persons, I'm talking about the legal term "right." William Stacy Johnson, a lawyer and theologian, writes that "the very notion of a 'right' is that it places limits on the arbitrary power of the majority.... If you have a right of free speech, you may exercise that right even if your speech happens to be offensive to the majority."†

So equal rights shouldn't be based on a vote. It is in fact *because* the majority of people do not support it that it should be a government-protected right. A "right" is the intentional limiting of the majority's power.

---

* If you want to know what the Bible really says, I talk about that some in *Fall to Grace,* and if you want to go deeper, read *A Time to Embrace* by William Stacy Johnson.

† William Stacy Johnson, *A Time to Embrace* (Grand Rapids, MI: Eerdmans Publishing Company, 2006), 11.

Christians should be the first people to recognize when someone's rights are being denied by the majority. In the kingdom of heaven, the oppressed are embraced, pursued, and accepted. The church should be on the front lines of the fight for the civil liberties of the oppressed.

3 This isn't a new issue for the church. In the first century, Paul tells us a story about the church having to deal with the "minority," which at that time was Gentiles in the church. The church was still Jewish, not a separate religion. When Paul and Peter meet at Antioch, Paul finds Peter a little confused on how to treat Gentile converts to the way of Jesus. The problem was that converts to Judaism, according to the Old Testament scriptures, were to be circumcised. But Paul claimed that circumcision was in direct opposition to grace.

Paul writes,

But when Cephas [Peter] came to Antioch, I opposed him to his face, because he stood self-condemned; for until certain people came from James, he used to eat with the Gentiles. But after they came, he drew back and kept himself separate for fear of the circumcision faction. And the other Jews joined him in this hypocrisy, so that even Barnabas was led astray by their hypocrisy. When I saw that they were not acting consistently with the truth of the gospel, I said to Cephas [Peter] before them all, "If you, though a Jew, live like a Gentile and not like a Jew, how can you compel the Gentiles to live like Jews?"*

My first thought is—what is Peter afraid of?

My second is—man, sometimes James seems like such an ass.†

4 A little background on Peter. He's a pretty impulsive guy, jumping out of boats to meet Jesus, confronting Jesus so vehemently that Jesus calls him "Satan." So we might expect some sort of behavior from Peter that shows he's not thinking things through.

But Peter is also this guy:

He became hungry and wanted something to eat; and while it was being prepared, he fell into a trance. He saw the heaven opened and something like a large sheet coming down, being lowered to the ground by its four corners. In it were all kinds of four-footed creatures and reptiles and birds of the air. Then he heard a voice saying, "Get up, Peter; kill and eat." But Peter said, "By no means,

---

* Galatians 2:11–14.

† If you don't believe me, reread chapter 5 in *Fall to Grace,* where I talk about the council in Acts where James somehow takes it upon himself to cherry-pick a few laws for the Gentile converts to follow.

Lord; for I have never eaten anything that is profane or unclean." The voice said to him again,
a second time, "What God has made clean, you
must not call profane."*

This vision isn't about food. Peter's hungry; he's
got food on his mind. But immediately after this,
Cornelius, a Gentile, calls to Peter. Peter's response?

"You yourselves know that it is unlawful for a
Jew to associate with or to visit a Gentile; but
God has shown me that I should not call anyone
profane or unclean."†

It's not about food; it's about people.

But then, seeing James's people walking around, Peter
backs down and starts following the law again.

So Paul comes up and says, "What's going on,
Peter?" And I'm sure that Peter's thinking, "Man,
between James and Paul, I just want to crawl into a
corner somewhere."

I understand Peter. It's hard to be a people-pleaser.
It's hard when you care what people think about what
you do and say. Even worse is to be a people-pleaser
and a radical; trust me, I know. I feel like I need to
speak out, set things straight, but I'm consumed with
making sure no one thinks I'm crazy for what I say.

---

*   Acts 10:10–15.

†   Acts 10:28.

I'll make a controversial statement, then sit watching the interwebs to see who criticizes me, and when they do, I feel terrible.

Peter was there when Jesus ate with sinners and tax collectors, and he heard all of Jesus's witty replies like "Those who are well have no need of a physician, but those who are sick."* But Peter was probably more like Homer Simpson or Tim Allen's character on *Home Improvement*; he tries to tell a story or say something profound but flubs it. "Sinners are sick, and you're not, and hospitals. Damn!"

5 Peter pulls away and gets scared of eating with Gentiles. Then others start segregating themselves, running back to the old way so much that Barnabas, who hung out with Paul, did it as well. And so Paul had to say something. He had to point out that Peter's actions were more than just hypocritical; they denied grace.

Paul couldn't stay silent, because legalism tears people apart. It brings shame and guilt when the Gospel is about freedom and grace.

You cannot be set free by legalism.

You cannot be transformed through the law.

You will not find grace by trying to follow the rules. There's nothing you can do. I can't say it enough. It's all grace.

---

* Matthew 9:12.

6 Peter's fear comes from *internal persecution* in the church. He is worried about the opinions of other leaders in the church. He's not worried about being caught by the Romans or the religious leaders. It's his own brothers* in Christ that are causing him to backtrack on the gospel of grace. It's James, a highly respected leader in the church, whom Peter fears.

It's the same today. We're all worried that if we speak out on certain unpopular issues, it's not those outside our community who would persecute us—it's those inside our community. You would think that relationships would be more important than theology, that community would be more important than belief. But unfortunately the church has a terrible track record of shooting its wounded and screaming at its dissidents.

People like James might inspire fear in others because deep down, they themselves are driven by fear. Fear of losing influence, fear of losing financial support. Fear of what people will say if they are seen eating and talking with outsiders, sinners, and outcasts. So they insulate themselves against people who are different. They protect themselves from "outsiders." They isolate themselves against other perspectives and ideas. All in the name of preserving or defending the truth.

But perhaps the truth is what they fear the most.

---

* We don't have evidence that his sisters in Christ were anywhere near so judgmental.

7 So Paul's saying to Peter here, "If you, though a Jew, live as a Gentile, how can you compel Gentiles to live as Jews?"

What he's saying is this: If you accept and receive grace, how can you treat others without grace? If you are welcomed and accepted simply because of grace, how can you not welcome and accept others because of that same grace?

I have a feeling that if I asked people if God loves gays, they'd say yes, but within seconds there would be some sort of qualification about how God feels about same-sex sexual behavior or even attraction. That's why I use *affirming*. There's no question where you stand when you are affirming.

William Stacy Johnson in his book *A Time to Embrace* talks about seven different stances toward same-sex attraction, ranging from prohibition to consecration. Most evangelical churches today assume the Bible is prohibitionist—which makes it difficult for anyone in their churches to take a different stance. Even those who accept LGBTQ persons as *people* still quickly qualify that their behavior, sexual orientation, or gender identity is unacceptable, and holding a position in leadership while openly LGBTQ is unacceptable. They hold that being gay is a tragic fate, and abstinence is their only choice.

But this doesn't work. It doesn't add up. As Johnson says, "This 'welcoming-but-not-affirming' policy is both self-contradictory and cruel. It is contradictory because it draws a distinction in theory that does not work in fact: to say to a person, 'I accept your sexual orientation, but I condemn you for acting upon it,' makes no sense either logically or practically.... Its effect is to heap judgment and shame on gay and lesbian people while at the same time withholding from them—and from their families—the love and support that heterosexual people take for granted. To be non-affirming is itself to be unwelcoming."*

If you're a Christian and your solution for gays and lesbians is "be celibate," pay attention here to Paul's words.

You who have received grace, how do you not extend grace?

8 So you've got James acting like the older, conservative, fundamentalist church. The Baptists, or Assemblies of God.† Peter's stuck in the middle, trying to be postmodern, but he's a nondenominational church plant from the fundamentalist church up the road. And Paul is the liberal, mainline denominations. The postmodern Lutheran, let's say.

That might not be helpful, but it's kind of funny to me.

What's most important about this early church experience is that the Gentiles are the outsiders. They're the ones that the church doesn't know how to accept. They don't follow the law. They don't conform to the

---

* William Stacy Johnson, *A Time to Embrace*, 71.

† Pick your own fundamentalist denomination if you don't like mine.

first-century Judean customs or rules or moralities. They don't fit in, they don't follow the rules, and their very presence in the community is scandalous to the first-century Christians. The first-century Christians would have considered them...*sinful.*

The church today seems to find these groups, the "sinners," everywhere.

Do you know who I'm talking about? Who would provoke scandalized looks in your church? A pregnant teen? Someone with piercings and tattoos? A woman preaching? A gay or lesbian couple? A homeless person? A Muslim? A transgender person? What sins does your church like to highlight in its sermons?

Or, better yet, what would ruin your reputation if you confessed it in front of the crowd?

We are all living by faith. We are all living under grace. The only difference between you and me and the "scandalous outsider" is nothing more than the labels we use to separate us from them.

9 Martin Luther King Jr. wrote that "we who engage in nonviolent direct action are not the creators of tension. We merely bring to the surface the hidden tension that is already alive."[*]

I've asked many if they are gay affirming, and this simple question provokes anger. I've yet to threaten

---

[*] Martin Luther King Jr., "Letter from a Birmingham Jail," accessed Oct. 20, 2012. http://www.africa.upenn.edu/Articles_Gen/Letter_Birmingham.html.

anyone, to say that if you don't answer, or don't say yes, I'm going to start spamming your email or send people to your house to break your legs. I ask, "Are you able to welcome and affirm LGBTQ people in your church?"

A few years ago I traveled with an organization called Soul Force on what they called the American Family Outing.* We spent over a year in preparation, calling and asking to meet with pastors and staff of American megachurches and have a meal with them and their families to talk about the issues facing LGBTQ Christians and their families. We faced a lot of opposition. People told us we were aggravators, we were just trying to get media attention. All we asked was to sit and have a meal.

If there's anything most anyone in the world can agree with when it comes to Jesus, it's that he shared meals with people. Specifically, with outsiders. Outcasts. Those who were hated, misunderstood, reviled in society. Some of the largest churches in the country were unwilling to share a meal with us. They couldn't sit down with people they disagreed with and have a conversation. They were too afraid that there'd be an *agenda*.

They acted like James, inspiring fear for those who don't get in line.

---

* I wrote about our attempted meeting with Rick Warren in *Fall to Grace*. In 2012 Rick Warren defended himself against accusations that arose when he ate a meal with Muslim leaders, met with them, traveled to Syria with them, and started a ministry to end misunderstandings with them. He couldn't share a meal with us, though. Jim Hinch, "Rick Warren builds bridge to Muslims," *The Orange County Register,* http://www.ocregister.com/articles/muslims-341669-warren-saddleback.html.

We weren't being agitators. We were just bringing to the surface the hidden tension that is already present in the contemporary evangelical church.

Why can't we sit down for a meal together, knowing we disagree? We find it easier to reach out to those of other faiths than those within our own faith. We insult each other from the pulpit and brag about conversions and attendance numbers.

There's a great Batman comic called *Knight and Squire*, about two British superheroes (the UK versions of Batman and Robin). In it, we meet all sorts of heroes and villains, including Jarvis Poker, the British Joker, who, instead of being a complete madman* like the Joker, is aging and sad and can't quite be bothered to make puns or jokes. In the world of *Knight and Squire* there's a pub called *The Time in a Bottle*, which is covered by an old magic dating back to the great wizard Merlin. No fighting or conflict can happen inside because of the truce magic. They can sit there and drink and take the piss out of one another, but they can't actually fight. They have to leave their battles at the door. You find villains and heroes sitting and talking. There might be tension. There might be arguments. But because they are unable to harm one another, they find friendship and mutual respect and community.

In the first episode of *Knight and Squire*, "For Six,"

---

* They say that the Joker exhibits "some kind of super-sanity" in *Arkham Asylum* by Grant Morrison and Dave McKean.

someone momentarily turns off the truce magic and a hero named Faceoff starts blasting at villains. Knight and Squire, Jarvis Poker, and the Milkman team up to protect the villains until the truce magic can be restored. Faceoff goes toe to toe with Knight and says, "You treat these villains like they're *people*."*

Imagine if people in the church could actually disagree but meet together for a drink or a meal. We could disagree and be civil at the same time. We could treat other Christians like *people*. I know: genius, right?

Instead, we shout and rail at each other from our bully pulpits, destroy and discount each other's entire ministries because of one political issue or one theological hair-split.

Paul warns in Galatians that if we bite and devour each other, we will be consumed. We need a pub like *The Time in a Bottle*. A place where the words we use to divide ourselves, to distinguish ourselves from one another—heretic and orthodox, liberal and conservative, biblical and unbiblical—aren't allowed. All we can do is sit and drink and talk. It's actually very simple. And it's a lot like Jesus. Jesus who engaged in theological discussion with a Pharisee under cover of night, with a Samaritan woman without a husband, and with the murderous crowd who had caught a woman in sin.

---

* Paul Cornell and Jimmy Broxton, "For Six: Part One," in *Knight and Squire* (New York: DC Comics, 2011).

10 This is sin on a level that most churches ignore. This is sin; meaning, that which destroys. That which is destructive, which causes hurt in other people and perhaps even in your own life. When people lose their jobs, aren't promoted, are discriminated against, are treated differently, are described as "gay" as an insult, get kicked out of churches, and are disowned by their families, that is sin. The non-affirmation of our LGBTQ brothers and sisters in the church is *destroying families*. Teens and adults are committing suicide because something they can't control and didn't choose is causing their friends and parents to reject them—at times with surprising violence—all in the name of God and holiness.

That is sin.

You know what sin is by what it does to people. Our rejection of those who don't fit within our clear-cut worldview is destroying people. Jesus said we would be known by our love, but when it comes to the LGBTQ community, we are known by our uncomfortable silence, our fight against their civil right to marry, our moral outrage, our discrimination, and our stereotyping.

11 So I'm asking people to ask their pastors and leaders, "Are we able to welcome and affirm LGBTQ people in our church?" This makes people angry, and I guess I understand.

Pastors and church leaders face much the same problem that politicians face. At first you get into ministry because you care, because you have ideals. You preach what you believe because of how much you believe it. But then things change; your beliefs shift when you study the Bible and open yourself up to conversation.

The problem is that people are used to their leaders saying things they agree with. The expectations of the people force pastors and leaders into silence. They become stuck with a theology that they don't buy into anymore and can't preach authentically because their congregation worships the idea of a manly God or a wealthy God or a vengeful God.

And those Gods demand sacrifice.

So many pastors choose to just go through the motions, do whatever it takes to keep the ministry going. My father, who was a pioneer of Christian television, told me once that his network had to stay on the air so they could keep raising money for the network to be on the air. It's like the ouroboros, the snake eating its own tail.

Paul and Jesus and Peter were all killed for what they believed, but pastors today would rather die than lose their financial support or fame. It's the new martyrdom—the assassination of your character.

So these pastors end up hunkering down with their people. They close themselves to the experience of learning and growing because they don't know how to lead their people into that same experience. They find themselves becoming defenders of their faith instead of pilgrims on a journey. And that causes them to turn on fellow Christians who are growing and exploring their faith. They are incapable of following them, and so, as Tillich writes, they become fanatics in order to repress their own need for questioning.

People say everyone's in process, that it takes time to make such a difficult change, to guide people into a new way of thinking. This sounds progressive and wise, but I wonder if it's just catering to the victimizers because we don't want to become victims ourselves. I know there are pastors and leaders who are affirming, but they don't say so because they're afraid that those who marginalize and ostracize gays and lesbians will set their sights on them.

They are afraid of their own brothers and sisters.

But do we want to be imprisoned by fear?

Is our reputation more important than the truth?

If we truly, really believed that the church should be welcoming and affirming of LGBTQ people, why would we hesitate to boldly proclaim the inclusiveness of the gospel?

12 So this is what gets me upset. We act as though our actions, especially our genitals and what we do with them, somehow make us acceptable to God. We've gotten so hung up now on sex that we'll ignore the character of God and the example of Jesus to declare war on those who don't fit our standard of sexual morality.

Is it really about their "sin"? Or is it about our fear that if we don't set ourselves apart from them that other Christians will see and judge us as outsiders as well?

For the majority of my life growing up, I worried about what other Christians would think. I didn't want them to think I wasn't a Christian, because they'd probably be right.

Jesus never worried about whom he was affiliated with. He hung around with society's so-called undesirables; he touched them, he forgave them, he talked with them, he ate with them, he pronounced that the kingdom of heaven belonged to them.

I had to learn that what other people think of me is their business. I had to learn that if I was going to follow Christ, I couldn't also follow other people.

13 I wouldn't be allowed to preach in the denomination I grew up in because I'm divorced. In the Assemblies of God, there were no questions asked and the reasons behind your divorce didn't matter, you were ineligible to preach. Done. Finished.

Forty years ago, it was interracial dating and marriage. Separate but equal. Bible verses were used to support that position. Remaining a pure people. Not mixing seeds. We look back now and think, That's crazy! Who could support that? Who could possibly think the Bible could be used to justify a ban on interracial dating? The answer is—we did. Christians. We sliced the Bible up and used verses out of context to defy the very nature of the Gospel.

Are we doing the same thing now?

You might be an activist for a group that has nothing to do with LGBTQ equality. You might be saying, "Jay, I can't sacrifice my ministry for this issue. I have a different calling."

But do you really?

Isn't our greatest calling to accept as we have been accepted?

Wouldn't your ministry be even greater if it were able to say that all are welcome? All are accepted?

14 The lyrics of the U2 song* "Sunday Bloody Sunday" ask, "How long must we sing this song?" How long before we stop calling it "sharing" instead of preaching when women are on the stage? How long will Sunday morning be the most segregated hour in America? How long are we going to cling to outdated notions of homosexuality and refuse to accept LGBTQ people into our midst? When are we going to finally live out the radical equality Paul talks about?

---

* For those of us old enough to listen to U2.

We don't have to be troublemakers, but it's not going to be comfortable for a while. The problem is already here; the tension is already under the surface. It's time to bring that tension to the surface and deal with it. I'm not becoming legalistic with the legalists. I'm taking responsibility for the opportunity I have to be a voice for equality, to end the intolerance and unacceptance of LGBTQ Christians.

My goal is for us to open our arms wide, not to nitpick. These issues have been nitpicked to death: women can be deacons but not elders, they can pray in church but not preach, gays are welcomed but not accepted, gays can have civil unions but not marriage. It makes me weary. My goal is to recognize that any grace that accepts me must accept everyone.

I don't want to be the person who says nothing. And so I'm going to keep talking.

Chapter 8

Seeking the Lost

In the end, we will remember not the words of our enemies but the silence of our friends.

—Martin Luther King Jr.

1 When I was a kid, my parents commissioned a bunch of paintings of Jesus—some for decoration, others people could order for a suggested donation to their ministry. One of these paintings—you can see it briefly in *One Punk Under God*—was based on Jesus's line "let the little children come to me."* Jesus is surrounded by little children, and if you look closely, one of the kids is me, and another is my sister.

Here's one of Jesus's encounters I've never seen in

---

* Mark 10:14.

paintings or stained glass or drawn along the hallway to Sunday school: "Now all the tax collectors and sinners were coming near to listen to him."* Not your typical, inspirational, Bible story scene: prostitutes and tax collectors and lepers all surrounding Jesus and listening to his teaching.

It made the religious leaders grumble, the writer of Luke goes on to tell us, "This fellow welcomes sinners and eats with them."†

This was Jesus's reputation around the synagogues. This is how Jesus was known. His great sin to the religious leaders was he not only welcomed sinners, but he *ate with them*. Eating a meal wasn't a casual social act in the culture at the time. It was a sign of respect to eat with someone; an affirmation of their dignity. The religious leaders grumbled that Jesus was validating those whom religion had invalidated through its laws and regulations.

When was the last time you got in trouble for eating with someone? Jesus was welcoming people who were unwelcome by the religious establishment, those considered immoral, unethical, sinful. The religious leaders thought that, by not allowing these people in, they were keeping themselves pure and holy and upright. They were protecting the sanctity of their religious institutions. They were taking back their culture for God, if you will.

---

* Luke 15:1.

† Luke 15:2.

But then Jesus came, and he spent time with the "undesirables." Welcomed them. Ate with them. They surrounded him and listened to his teaching. He took the notion of "who's in and who's out" and turned it on its head by making the "in" people the "out" people, and vice versa.

The Pharisees and scribes were concerned about who was in and who was out, who was worthy to share a meal and who wasn't, who was forgiven and unforgiven, who was loved and unloved. But Jesus had a better way, and immediately after the religious leaders grumble, Jesus tells them a series of parables.

The lost sheep.

The lost coin.

The lost son.

Let's take a look at these stories and see why Jesus chose to tell them to the church leaders of his day.

2 So he told them this parable:

Which one of you, having a hundred sheep and losing one of them, does not leave the ninety-nine in the wilderness and go after the one that is lost until he finds it? When he has found it, he lays it on his shoulders and rejoices. And when he comes home, he calls together his friends and neighbors, saying to them, "Rejoice with me, for

I have found my sheep that was lost." Just so, I tell you, there will be more joy in heaven over one sinner who repents than over ninety-nine righteous persons who need no repentance.*

The shepherd leaves the ninety-nine in the wilderness† to go look for the lost one. It's funny that Jesus says "which one of you does *not* leave the ninety-nine" because it's not the best move to leave ninety-nine percent of your flock wandering in the wilderness to find one. I'd be worried about the sheep I still had, not the one I lost. You would think that *none* of them would leave the ninety-nine.

It seems like Jesus's shepherd isn't doing what makes sense.

Instead, he's on a radical mission.

One that could cost him everything.

3 The story of the lost coin is similar.

Or what woman having ten silver coins, if she loses one of them, does not light a lamp, sweep the house, and search carefully until

---

* Luke 15:3–7. I've actually heard preachers upping the ante on this one, saying that when finding a lost sheep, a shepherd breaks its legs so it won't ever get lost again. Not only is that freaky, it's nowhere in this story. Sorry, folks.

† Some translations say "hill," but I think it's more dramatic when it's "wilderness," as in the NRSV.

she finds it? When she has found it, she calls together her friends and neighbors, saying, "Rejoice with me, for I have found the coin that I had lost."*

I think Jesus is telling his own story here. His story of welcoming and eating with sinners and tax collectors. Jesus wouldn't be worried about what his congregation would think. He wouldn't be concerned about where the money was going to come from, or how many donors they would lose. He isn't thinking that the sheep will eventually wander back or the coin will somehow turn up, if you just wait long enough.

Instead, he says that the angels in heaven rejoice more over this one person than they do over ninety-nine who don't need to be welcomed and accepted.

I've gotten in trouble for encouraging the church to be welcoming and affirming of those the church has traditionally deemed "outsiders." Some have even said I was bragging and trying to decide a new "in" or "out" based on a church's stance on this issue. That's not what I'm doing. I see it more like the woman here who calls together her friends and neighbors and says, "Rejoice with me!" I want people to speak out. Those who are tired of the walls the church has built must speak up and not be afraid of what people think. I want them to raise their voices and let the church know that tribalism is unacceptable. To raise their voices to let

---

* Luke 15:8–9.

those the church has marginalized know that they are loved, welcomed, accepted, and affirmed in Christ.

The truth is, if you're silent, you're just as responsible as the oppressors. If you're not saying anything, you're enabling the oppression. Martin Luther King Jr. said in his *Letter from a Birmingham Jail*:

> We know through painful experience that freedom is never voluntarily given by the oppressor; it must be demanded by the oppressed. Frankly, I have yet to engage in a direct action campaign that was "well timed" in the view of those who have not suffered unduly from the disease of segregation. For years now I have heard the word "Wait!"...this "Wait" has almost always meant "Never." We must come to see, with one of our distinguished jurists, that "justice too long delayed is justice denied."*

My church in Atlanta had a church, a staff, a grant, a ministry to people. The church and I had a lot to lose if what I said displeased the financial base of the church. My staff would lose their jobs. Our funding would be cut off. Attendance would drop. This happens often to leaders in the church: people want to please their manly God or their heterosexual God or

---

* Martin Luther King Jr., "Letter from a Birmingham Jail," accessed Oct. 20, 2012. http://www.africa.upenn.edu/Articles_Gen/Letter_Birmingham.html.

their wealthy God or their liberal God, and their leaders had better not break down the tribal walls to their God. They want their leaders to erect walls in honor of their God.

I stood to lose staff, money, ministry, everything if I spoke up for gay, lesbian, transgender, bi, and queer Christians, and I held back, until one day I realized that none of that mattered. I said the Bible has been abused, has been used to justify discrimination, and that it was wrong to do so. I said that they are loved and accepted, and that from now on I would be preaching grace that includes them, not excludes them.

And I lost everything I thought I'd lose. But it didn't matter, because I freed myself from the burden of indifference.

4 And in freeing myself, I found the true calling of the church, the counter-cultural, revolutionary nature of the Gospel.

The church should be a community of invitation.

The church should be a community of affirmation.

The church should be a community of restoration.

The church should not be a community where we are afraid to open the arms of God's grace ever wider.

The church should not be a community where we are afraid to speak up for the outsider.

If we believe Martin Luther King Jr.'s words, the

silence of those who are affirming is more damaging than the loud protests of the non-affirming.

Many of my LGBTQ friends are tired of being compared to the lost sheep or the lost coin or considered the "sick" person (when Jesus says that it is the sick who need a doctor). I get that. It's important to understand, though, that Jesus is talking to the Pharisees with these three parables. He's rebuking them in language that speaks to them. To them, the "sinners and tax collectors" are lost sheep, lost coins, lost sons. To them, these people are inherently outsiders.

But look what Jesus is doing. He's turning the "outsiders" into *the prized possession*. Angels and neighbors and owners rejoice, not over the ninety-nine sheep or the nine coins, but over the one who is welcomed. Jesus is painting a picture of a God who cares about those marginalized by society and by the church.

Jesus is telling the Pharisees that the person the church sees as "sinner"—cast out, condemned, devalued—is the one God sees as "saint"—welcomed, affirmed, prized.

5 After the lost sheep and the lost coin, Jesus tells the story of the prodigal son. I love this story, and I've preached about it and written about it before. I'm going to write about it again. It's that good.

Then Jesus said, "There was a man who had two sons. The younger of them said to his father, 'Father, give me the share of the property that will belong to me.'"*

I want you to fully realize how offensive this statement is. This isn't like asking for your allowance a week early. This is saying, in effect, I wish you were dead. I no longer want to have anything to do with this family. This is a severe disgrace to the family, and so Jesus's listeners are already caught off guard, because the father agrees and divides his property for his son.

Then the son takes his money and "squanders his property in dissolute living."† After losing all his property, a famine strikes the land, and the son is left feeding pigs and coveting the pigs' food. This is possibly the lowest a person could get in that society—coveting the food of pigs.

The son isn't someone with the purest motives to come back home. He's hungry, broke, living in an economy filled with hungry and broke people, and he thinks, "I'll just go back to Dad." So he figures out the best way to get his father to accept him back again: "'I will say to him, "Father, I have sinned against heaven

---

* Luke 15:11–12.

† Luke 15:13.

and before you; I am no longer worthy to be called your son; treat me like one of your hired hands.' "'*

I would come home sometimes after curfew as a kid, sneaking through the door in the dark, and my mom—who wasn't even five feet tall—would be sitting, rocking slowly in a chair, and in a low, menacing tone she would say, *"Where have you been?"*

What was I going to tell her? I'd been out squandering money. I'd been hanging out with my friends for an extra hour and didn't want to call. I'd been drinking.

(Then Mom would say, "Have you been drinking?" I remember saying yes once, and she said she was going to pray that the next time I drank I would get sicker than I've ever been sick before. Um, thanks?)

That's what I'd expect this father to say. *Where have you been?*

But while he was still far off, his father saw him and was filled with compassion; he ran and put his arms around him and kissed him.[†]

And when the son finally performs his speech, he only gets a phrase or two out before he's interrupted by the father saying to his slaves:

---

*   Luke 15:18–19.

†   Luke 15:20.

"Quickly, bring out a robe—the best one—and put it on him; put a ring on his finger and sandals on his feet. And get the fatted calf and kill it, and let us eat and celebrate; for this son of mine was dead and is alive again; he was lost and is found!"*

Not *where have you been?*
Not *have you been drinking?*
Not *what did you do with all of my money?*

Not stomping his feet, pounding the podium, or not meeting his gaze, uncomfortable with the idea of this sinner even being welcomed back as a slave, let alone a son.

The father does the same thing that the shepherd and the woman have done before him—he rejoices and calls all of his friends to rejoice. Jesus goes beyond a wandering sheep or a misplaced coin and paints what might have been for his hearers the worst possible picture. This is a rebellious son, having disgraced his family by squandering his fortune on immoral living and returning only when it served his self-interest.

But this son, rather than being punished, lectured, required to make restitution, or asked to make a list of all his faults, is celebrated, welcomed, robed in the finest garment, and declared to be loved and accepted.

It's a beautiful story.

---

* Luke 15:22–24.

6

But it's not the end of the story, because it turns out this guy has a big brother.

Now his elder son was in the field; and when he came and approached the house, he heard music and dancing. He called one of the slaves and asked what was going on. He replied, "Your brother has come, and your father has killed the fatted calf, because he has got him back safe and sound." Then he became angry and refused to go in. His father came out and began to plead with him. But he answered his father, "Listen! For all these years I have been working like a slave for you, and I have never disobeyed your command; yet you have never given me even a young goat so that I might celebrate with my friends. But when this son of yours came back, who has devoured your property with prostitutes, you killed the fatted calf for him!" Then the father said to him, "Son, you are always with me, and all that is mine is yours. But we had to celebrate and rejoice, because this brother of yours was dead and has come to life; he was lost and has been found."*

What if the father had said to the older brother: "*You're right.* I didn't think of it that way. Wow—whores

---

* Luke 15:25–32.

and prostitutes? I didn't know *that*. What will people say? We'll have to get him to publicly denounce all that or else people will get the wrong idea. Tell him to come back once he's ready to pay back all that he wasted and after he's lived clean for a while."

Or what if the father, instead of ordering his servants to robe the son and throw a party, had said to his returning son: "Listen, I'm glad you're here and all, and I would totally throw a party for you, but I think your brother is going to get kind of pissed if we do. So act like a slave for a while and we'll slowly get people used to the idea of you being back around, and I'll eventually give you this ring and a nice cloak but it'll take some time."

I used to ask myself: Who am I? Am I the prodigal? Or am I the older son? The prodigal is humble and contrite; the older son, proud and vain. But I don't think that's what we're supposed to get from this story. It's not about identifying as the younger or older brother. It's about being like the father, who accepts them both. It's about welcoming the legalistic son and the crazy wild son both into your family. It's saying I want you both in my presence. I don't want to lose either of you.

The one son gets a party. The older brother says it's not fair. That, again, is the beautiful thing about grace. You're forgiven. You're accepted. You're searched out, brought back, welcomed, and thrown a party.

*　　*　　*

Jesus is saying that when someone's not around, when somebody's missing, you leave everyone and go find them. You leave everyone in the wilderness if you must, because it's more important to find that one person who isn't around. They need to be welcomed in, they need to know that they are a part of this family, this community. They are welcome. The community isn't complete until they come home. When they're gone, something just isn't right.

Neither the shepherd nor the woman nor the father ever give up. They keep looking until they find what they are looking for. They are willing to give up everything else to make sure that one person is welcomed back in.

This is such a contrast to the church that commits to disciplining those they consider "lost" and refusing them fellowship with the other members of the church. Instead of sending out letters on how to excommunicate someone, we should be sending out letters on how to *drop everything to find this person and welcome them back.*

This is a beautiful thing, to give up everything to find the lost one.

But what if you come back and half of the ninety-nine are gone? I don't know. I love that Jesus doesn't even say they thought about that. The fact is, you go. You find the lost sheep. You clean the whole house. You run out to meet your son.

7 There's a similar story Jesus tells in the book of Luke that I've written and talked about before. This story is a response to someone asking Jesus how to get eternal life. Jesus allows the man to answer his own question—love God and love your neighbor—and then tells the man to go and do that. Wanting to test him, the man says, "Who is my neighbor?"

> Jesus replied, "A man was going down from Jerusalem to Jericho, and fell into the hands of robbers, who stripped him, beat him, and went away, leaving him half dead. Now by chance a priest was going down that road; and when he saw him, he passed by on the other side. So likewise a Levite, when he came to the place and saw him, passed by on the other side. But a Samaritan while traveling came near him; and when he saw him, he was moved with pity. He went to him and bandaged his wounds, having poured oil and wine on them. Then he put him on his own animal, brought him to an inn, and took care of him. The next day he took out two denarii, gave them to the innkeeper, and said, 'Take care of him; and when I come back, I will repay you whatever more you spend.' "*

A priest passes by him, a Levite passes by, but a

---

* Luke 10:30–35.

Samaritan stops and helps the man, taking care of him and paying for his care. The difference between the priest and the Samaritan is that the Samaritan isn't thinking "What will happen to me if I stop?" but "What will happen to this man if I don't stop?"

Maybe the priest isn't thinking about himself. Maybe he's thinking of all the people where he's headed and that they won't receive him if he's unclean because he touched what looks like a dead body. Perhaps he's thinking, in a sense, of his congregation. If he stops for this person, what will happen to all the other people he's on his way to minister to?

I hadn't thought of it this way until I encountered such anger when I encouraged people to ask their leaders if they were gay affirming. "We need time," the leaders said. "You can't rush this kind of change," they said. "We've worked really hard to build this ministry. If we help on this issue, all the people who work here might lose their jobs, not just me." Or, "People might stop supporting my ministry. What will happen to all these other people if we go and help this one person over here?"

Are those good excuses? Can we turn away from the half-dead man because there are dozens more needing our help somewhere else? It doesn't matter what the good intentions of the priest or the Levite were, there was a person dying on the side of the road. Nothing else mattered.

This is the countercultural revolution that we find in Jesus. This is a main reason I have found myself drawn to what Jesus called the kingdom of heaven. Over and over, Jesus demonstrated God's abandonment of the privileged and pursuit of the oppressed. If we aren't doing this—actively, radically, with abandon—then are we really following Christ?

If we can't drop everything to help someone in pain, if we can't leave the ninety-nine in order to rescue this one lost sheep, then what good are we? What kind of love can we claim to have when we silently stand by while other Christians are shaming and mocking a group of people and fighting against their civil rights simply because of their sexuality or gender—or age or race or economic status or social status or anything else? If we help someone feel loved and accepted, if we help the church become a safe place for all, if we stop someone's hurt and pain, then and only then are we a part of the kingdom of heaven.

8 It makes sense for the rebellious son to be turned away. It makes sense to stick with the ninety-nine sheep who are obeying orders. It makes sense to wait to see if the coin just turns up on its own. It makes sense for the Levite and priest to pass by the beaten, half-dead man.

But the beautiful thing is that the Samaritan stops, the woman sweeps, the shepherd leaves the ninety-nine. And the father goes out of his way to restore his son, not by requiring the son to do anything, but simply by affirming and celebrating the son for nothing more than the fact that *he is the father's son*.

There's no other qualification.

We don't know what happens to the ninety-nine sheep. We don't know if the older brother finally gets on board and joins the party. All we have is the father pleading with the older brother, saying, "Come in. I love you. I can't force you to come in, but everything that is mine has always been yours, and so come and join the fun. Let's show your brother grace. Let's show him compassion. Let's open ourselves up to a greater life, a better life, where both my sons are accepted and loved. Come celebrate with us."

The choice before us now is this: Will we stop and help the person on the side of the road? Will we leave the ninety-nine to embrace the one? Will we embrace the younger son and throw him a huge party, welcoming him home? Will we sweep the house, every corner, until the broom is worn and useless?

If your church opens arms of grace wider than you are comfortable with—much like the older brother in the prodigal son story—and you no longer want to be a part of that expanded community, I plead with you: Come on in. We love you. We can't force you to come in, but we can offer you the opportunity to live a better life where you, too, can join the party that we are throwing for those who were lost to us.

If you are affirming, but your church hasn't opened their doors to LGBT individuals, do not be silent. You will encounter resistance. You might be branded as a troublemaker. You might lose money, friends, or become unwelcome at your church. But silence is more costly, because you are ignoring the commands of the father: Go! Fetch the finest robe! Kill the fatted calf! Throw a party! Rejoice with me!

Chapter 9

Opening Up the Church Doors

The universe is God's sanctuary. Every work day is a day of the Lord, every supper a Lord's supper, every work the fulfillment of a divine task, every joy a joy in God.

—*Paul Tillich,* The Church and Contemporary Culture

1 I remember one time going to the Guggenheim, the art museum in New York City that is shaped in a spiral, almost like a parking garage. We were within thirty feet from the top, with only a few paintings left to see, when suddenly a group of security guards herded us down the spiral hallways. We were told we couldn't go up any farther, we had to head out the doors so they could close. We asked, but they just wouldn't let us see the last five paintings.

We often treat church, it seems, like a museum, a God gallery. We go to a museum to experience art. We don't find it on a street corner—we find it in a gallery. You give a suggested donation to keep the place in business; art has to survive on charity. You don't want to be there too long, looking at art on the walls. Learning about the history of art can get tedious. You feel like you should know something about art, though. When you leave, you leave art behind. Art is for museums, you think.

In the same way, the church service has become a place where you come, observe spiritual things, perhaps even get excited about them, but eventually the doors close and you have to go. You get a sermon to take home with you, you get maybe a song stuck in your head, just like buying a print at the museum gift shop. But then you're home.

It's an unnatural experience of God, just like the gallery is an unnatural experience of art. The gallery collects all the art in one place, tries to draw you in, and then tries to get you to keep coming back. It tries to balance art viewing with "fun" exhibits, mixing contemporary pieces with older, historical art so you will view both. People who donate get special benefits, tickets, and viewing times. It becomes less about the art and more about the marketing and donation efforts.

The church does the same thing. "God is here in this place" or "We're standing on holy ground." I heard these a lot as a kid. "Can't you just feel God's presence?"

We stuff all of our spiritual activities into one space. We sing worshipful, moving, reverent songs. We have profound experiences. We send our children to be educated in Sunday school about Bible stories. We listen to the Word of God and expect to be moved by powerful testimony and intelligent, informed interpretation of scripture. We want coffee and donuts either before or afterward. It's like McDonald's: fast-food faith. You drive through to get what you need in the shortest time possible. You sit down and expect sports on the TV, a play place for the kids, free wi-fi, happy meals, coffee, and a bagel in the narthex.

In other words, we want to be fed.

2 Jesus actually said something about that.

John 4 says Jesus has to go* through Samaria on his way from Judea to Galilee, and arriving at a city, Jesus rests by a well. A Samaritan woman comes to draw water and Jesus asks her for a drink. They have a long exchange, one that sounds suspiciously like one a rabbi would have with his disciple. They talk about living water, worshiping neither in a temple nor on a mountain, but "in spirit and truth." He tells the woman about her many former husbands and that man she lives with to whom she is not

---

* I think it's fascinating that the Bible says he "had to go" or "was compelled to go" through Samaria. Normally they would travel around Samaria to avoid dealing with Samaritans. But Jesus had to go through. He had to speak with this woman, to minister to the Samaritans.

married, but he does not condemn her. Instead, he makes her his first disciple in this city, and because the woman's testimony intrigued the local Samaritans, they invite him to stay for two more days.

In the midst of this story, Jesus's disciples arrive and urge him to eat something. "But he said to them, 'I have food to eat that you do not know about.' So the disciples said to one another, 'Surely no one has brought him something to eat?' Jesus said to them, 'My food is to do the will of him who sent me and to complete his work.'"*

3 Jesus was being fed. That's what we expect from church, right? But his church, then, was happening at a well talking with a woman about the crap in her life and how God is always right there, not on a mountain or in a temple.

What if that's it? What if the real purpose of church is to remind us that everything we do is a spiritual activity? Pastors often tell their congregations that they can't just be Christians on Sunday morning and then live like an "unbeliever" the rest of the week. The rest of the week, Christians ought to be more like they are on Sunday morning, they say.

I think it's the opposite. Sunday morning ought to be more like the rest of the week.

---

* John 4:32–34.

4 If God is everywhere and not just in church, why do we hear so much about God "showing up" or God "making his presence known"? Especially during worship music, it seems as if we use language designed to somehow bring "more" of God in our midst. It's one of the reasons why, at the church where I am co-pastor, we don't sing together. Singing is not wrong, and I'm not against worship music. It's just too tempting to believe that the emotions you feel during the music somehow conjure up the divine. In the mall, in the bathroom, in our deepest, darkest moments, God is there. Why would God show up more when I sing a song with a group of people rather than when I'm at a bar having a conversation? I experience God and feel the presence of the divine during that conversation. Not during a song—but in the crazy moments of ordinary life, the encounters, conversations, and relationships we have throughout our whole lives.

5 Perhaps church could be more like an art appreciation class. You could come to church and learn how to appreciate God in the everyday, how to find God in the rest of the world, not just on Sundays.

This is why I don't really teach much on Sunday mornings. We might look at the scripture and figure out what it means to live out vulgar, radical, offensive grace in that world, but it's not teaching. It's expressing that God's love is wider and broader and greater than anyone's ever told us. It's saying that what people have asked you to sacrifice aren't really the things that you should be sacrificing. It's about refocusing on grace and love. It's making the world a safe place for all people.

You ought to be able to come to church with faith or no faith. You should be accepted no matter what—and hopefully that gives you the opportunity and the appreciation for how you can love and accept others in your life.

I want people to understand grace in their everyday life. I want them to know they're accepted every moment of their life. I want them to experience God—*every moment*. I want them to know that they're loved, they're accepted, and they can love and accept others because of that. Everything else is gravy.

6 Our church in Brooklyn meets in a bar. The service can only be an hour because the bar hosts an open mic afterward. After church, we head out to the bar and just sit around and talk. Members belong to our church simply by staying around to talk to other people. We encourage community, meaning we want people to communicate. Usually churches do that through "membership," which inevitably comes with rules and regulations. (Some churches take it even further, into contract signing and submission to discipline.) But membership is not community.

In New York City, Brooklyn especially, people are moving constantly. The first way we try to make church not follow the art gallery model is to tell people: This isn't your only community. Your primary community is where you live. Where you shop. Who you spend time with. That's where you find faith. That's where you find God. Those are the people who will stick with you and that you can rely on and share with and love.

The art gallery church wants to be the community—shop with us, do your hair with us, hang out with us. You end up with members constantly at the art gallery church, forgetting the rest of their life. They forget that their coworkers, the cashier at the coffee shop, and the street musician are their community too. Churches end up insulated, with churchgoers unaware of how to discover art in the streets instead of in the gallery; how to see God in their daily lives.

We should be more like *Sesame Street*. There's Muppets. There's people. There's music playing in one corner and a tire swing on the other side. *Sesame Street* teaches us that our tribe doesn't just include the people we agree with or the people who look like us. Our tribe includes birds and grouches and counts and characters of all shapes and sizes and colors. They are the people in our lives, everywhere. Who are the people in your neighborhood? They're the people that you meet each day.

7 One of the best parts of my life in Atlanta was the time I spent working at the record store in the hip shopping area. The people working at the shops in that area were my community. My family. We spent holidays together when one of us didn't have a place to go. And it wasn't about getting these people to come to my church. I didn't care if they ever came to my church. The church service was just something I did—it wasn't as important as just living my life with friends and family.

In these big churches where the pastor isn't really there, where they are more worried about getting their message or theology out rather than caring for or being a part of a community, they can't even be normal people. When pastors hole up in buildings surrounded by huge lawns and parking lots, we miss out on community. It's amazing how quickly you lose touch if you're always in a Bible study and everybody's always talking about Jesus and Christianity. You see everything through this filter of God and Satan, of spiritual and secular. Us and them. You create your own insulated world. When we hear mega-church preachers say something that seems out of touch with reality, we have to understand that they don't live in the real world. Christians create a false world, one without the people that Jesus cared about.

This is in some ways understandable. If we really

did have an all-inclusive church, it would be a very uncomfortable place. Accepting everyone doesn't mean we're all comfortable, it doesn't mean "I'm okay, you're okay." It means we're a community, we're looking out for each other, and at times I will need to sit down with my brother and say, "I don't get this part about you," and that the church will be a safe place for that to happen.

It's not easy. I know this personally. I'm an introvert, a recluse, a pessimist. This stuff is hard for me. It doesn't come easily. But it is the right thing to do.

8 When it comes to the church, we need to rip the art off the walls and hang it up all around town. We need to rid the church of what makes it feel like a God gallery and move more toward an appreciation class. How to find God in the everyday, instead of trying to "produce" God for a Sunday morning experience.

We need to open the doors of the church, not to let other people in, but to get ourselves out. Instead of having Wednesday night church, let's give people ideas on how to spend time as a family on Wednesday nights. Give people a recipe for an easy meal, a game idea,* and have a night where everyone in the church invites their neighbors over for game night—or invites them out to a night of the great American

---

* Uno Attack. That's my favorite.

sport of bowling. Pick a local store and support it with your business. Frequent your local coffee shop and get to know the baristas.

When Jesus wanted to be fed, he *did* something. He didn't expect someone to feed him. He fed himself. He got out there and talked with people—scandalous people. A Samaritan? A woman? A divorced woman living with another man? And what's he doing— engaging her in theological discourse? All of these things are radically inclusive. He's not converting her, correcting her, confronting her. He's showing her that she is not only accepted and loved but also respected and valued.

Don't invite people to church; invite yourself to leave the church and find the people.

Chapter 10

Becoming the Outcast

Truly I tell you, the tax collectors and the prostitutes
are going into the kingdom of God ahead of you.

—Matthew 21:31

1 *The Village*, a 2004 movie directed by M. Night
Shyamalan (who is famous for his mind-blowing
twists at the end of his movies), depicts a community of nineteenth-century villagers afraid of monsters in the surrounding woods. Something terrible is
out there, and the town is the only safe place. Kids
aren't allowed to go beyond a certain distance. Sometimes they put an animal out in the forest to appease
the monster. And sometimes the people would even
get glimpses of the monster in the woods.

And it turns out, it's all fake. There's nothing out in the woods. It's actually a community of adults who left the outside world to create their own secluded society. They invent the myth of monsters to keep their kids from entering the world, and they even dress up as the monster so the kids will believe the lie. And it's not the nineteenth century, either. It's present day. Bam. Blew your mind.

Sometimes I think the church today is operating under a similar mind-set as the adults in *The Village*, so afraid of "the world" that they set up rules and lines and boundaries in order to safeguard their worldview. But what the movie shows us is that, in order to protect the people, the parents had to become the monsters. They had to become that which would keep the people in fear. Perhaps this is why so many people use the word "escaping" when they talk about leaving the church.

Eastern University professor and blogger Peter Enns writes about how evangelical seminaries are sheltering their students from certain "dangerous" modes of thought. He quotes a seminary professor who explains to his former student, "Our job was to protect you from this information so as to not ship-wreck your faith."[*]

This "protection" isn't real life. Sharon Baker puts it this way:

---

[*] Peter Enns, "If They Only Knew What I Thought: The Sad Cycle of Evangelical Biblical Scholarship," accessed August 2012. http://www.patheos.com/blogs/peterenns/2012/06/if-they-only-knew-what-i-thought-the-sad-cycle-of-evangelical-biblical-scholarship/.

We believe that hell, with its eternal violence, is necessary to protect the community, God's community, from violence and unrighteousness. The hell myth exists as the very fabric of our perspective on God's last judgment.... We insist that God designed it all, that behind all the torment and torture lies God, the very God who loves enemies.... We believe that the victims... pervert our Christian community and deserve the punishment they receive.*

Most of the tactics used by the church to control people have their root in fear. Neither fear nor control is good news.

Word is starting to get out, especially since the Internet allows people to broadcast publicly when they are being shamed and abused by churches. Some churches have elaborate "discipline" processes that are now being revealed by people they've forced through this process. Most every time I read about abusive discipline like this or talk to someone who has gone through it, Matthew 18 is brought up. It's like the anti–First Corinthians 13. It's worth taking a look at this passage and the idea of "discipline" in the church.

"If another member of the church sins against you, go and point out the fault when the two of you are alone. If the member listens to you,

---

* Sharon L. Baker, *Razing Hell,* chapter 5.

you have regained that one. But if you are not listened to, take one or two others along with you, so that every word may be confirmed by the evidence of two or three witnesses. If the member refuses to listen to them, tell it to the church; and if the offender refuses to listen even to the church, let such a one be to you as a Gentile and a tax collector.*

I think the most important thing to do here is interpret this passage in light of Jesus's own actions. Because when churches use Matthew 18, they are justifying telling the entire church about someone's sin and then commanding members of the church to refuse to talk to or associate with them (often detailing exactly what kind of activities and conversations are appropriate or inappropriate). This supposedly comes from the line "let such a one be to you as a Gentile and a tax collector."

Treat that person like a tax collector. This is heavy irony here, because in whose name is this gospel written? Matthew. Tax collector. And man called by Jesus to follow him, whom Jesus brought into his inner circle of ministry without any repentance process, intervention, or confrontation. Jesus was constantly criticized for eating with and associating with tax collectors and Gentiles. When Jesus shared meals and kept company with these people, it was scandal-

---

*   Matthew 18:15–17.

ous because he was saying, "These are my people." It's difficult to justify excommunication because of Matthew 18, when just by saying "Matthew 18" you're naming the tax collector embraced by Jesus.

Jesus also says, "If the member listens to you, you have regained that one." Imagine the reaction if a pastor went to his or her board of elders and said, "I blew it. This is what happened. I'm sorry. Let's deal with it." And the board said, "We're glad you came to us. We've won you back. We're done with it. Taken care of. Done."

Most churches would cry out, "That's not justice, Jay. They have to step down from leadership and go through years of recovery." That's what churches do to leaders who have fallen.

But Jesus called tax collectors and zealots to be his disciples, and not after a long restoration process. He told them to come follow him immediately.

In fact, Jesus talked with all sorts of people without confronting them about their sin and demanding repentance. And we don't have any stories of Jesus using the Matthew 18 process with any of them.

2 In light of the whole of the New Testament, if you don't agree with someone's lifestyle or choices or identity, ignoring them or disassociating with them is the least Christian thing you can do. To say that you can't be in my wedding, or I won't be in your wedding, or for a church not to allow someone to attend, or volunteer, or serve because they don't agree with their relationships, lifestyle, choices, or identity is wrong.

I once kept someone from volunteering at our church, and they took me aside and said, "Jay, this goes against everything you preach about grace—you're full of shit."

They were right. I was being selective. How do I expect to have community with someone when I say you can't help me, but I can help you? That's saying, I'm better than you, and so much better that I won't even accept your help.

That's not Jesus.

That's control.

We've been raised in a culture that believes that the bad apple is going to destroy life as we know it. "It becomes more important to root out evil than to promote good," Richard Holloway writes. "Contrary to the words of Jesus in the parable of the tares and wheat, when he told us to let both grow together till the harvest, much energy is spent pulling out weeds from the Church's fields."*

If people were to drink and get wasted, then go to an AA meeting, you know how they're going to stay sober? By volunteering their ass off at AA. Make coffee before the meeting and put up the chairs after the meeting. Focusing on the other people takes their

---

* Holloway, *Doubts and Loves,* chapter 15.

mind off of their own problems and gives them the freedom to work through their issues.

If you go out and have a drink, AA's *not* going to ask you not to come back. They're not going to say, "Sorry, you can't come in here. Come back when you are sober." Instead, you enter, and they give you a white chip and say, "You've got today." You can walk into a meeting within five minutes of your last drink. There's no punishment process. No discipline process. You're welcomed in and offered the opportunity to do what works. In AA, the only requirement is the desire to not drink. There are no rules, just recommendations.

Jesus shows us an example of reconciliation with Peter.

> When they had finished breakfast, Jesus said to Simon Peter, "Simon son of John, do you love me more than these?" He said to him, "Yes, Lord; you know that I love you." Jesus said to him, "Feed my lambs."[*]

There's no apology, no confession; he just responds sheepishly[†] to Jesus and affirms his love for him three times. That's it. No contract. No discipline. Just restoration.

---

[*] John 21:15.

[†] Pun definitely intended. They call me the Pun-isher.

3 It's also important to read Matthew 18 in light of the surrounding verses. Immediately after, Jesus tells Peter to forgive not seven but seventy-seven times. And then he tells a story about the unforgiving servant—a story that promotes forgiving as we have been forgiven. Right before this passage is the parable of the lost sheep.

The point of Matthew 18—the whole chapter, not just the famous "discipline" part—is *restoration*.

I was raised with a view of this God who needs a sacrifice, who needs blood to forgive, but then Jesus comes along talking about grace. Jesus gives us a radically new way to approach being wronged. He says, can you go any further to forgive people? If you can, do that. Seek them out. Don't keep a tally. Remember you've been forgiven. If you can't restore them, still eat with them, talk with them, and spend time with them, as Jesus did with the tax collectors and Gentiles. These are radical ideas of Jesus. Radical ideas of grace. We are called to be forgivers and restorers. Go to them again. Then go to them again. Don't wait for them to come to you, and don't cut them off. Go to them again.

4 This is not just a Matthew 18 theme. Richard Holloway writes that throughout his life, Jesus "placed himself and God on the side of those the official system defined as expendable outcasts, among whom he generated an excitement about this new understanding of God. He did more than question the received order: he treated it as though it did not exist; he acted as if his own vision of the welcoming father were already a universal reality."* This means that the moment a church casts someone out, they align that person with Jesus and cast themselves in the role of "the official system." Notice that the difference between the system and Jesus is that Jesus saw no one as expendable, no one as an outcast. When the church decides that people are less important than programs, they have become the system.

The church has protected itself from this truth by looking at the stories of Jesus interacting with the official religious system of his day through rose-colored glasses. When Jesus rebukes the Pharisees and welcomes the prostitute, it seems so obvious to us who was *really* in and who was *really* out. We've twisted these stories, vilified the Pharisees. The Pharisees are always bad guys, with the evil voices and ominous tones, and we think of the tax collectors as these poor, misunderstood sinners that Jesus hung out with because they were so persecuted by these evil religious leaders. We justify looking around today and saying that today's outcasts really should be outcasts and that we really aren't as bad as those Pharisees. We justify our own prejudices.

But the Pharisees were the open-minded thinkers

---

* Holloway, *Doubts and Loves,* chapter 11.

of their day. They thought that perhaps there was life after death, and they had other mind-boggling ideas. They were respectable and upstanding leaders. Think of them like you would a successful business owner or the founder of a charity.

And then you had tax collectors. I can't communicate how vile that phrase would sound to the Judeans of Jesus's day. Tax collectors were Judeans, but they were in league with the oppressors, the Romans. They could take whatever money you had on you as a tax to the government, and so the everyday person would look down and refuse to meet the eyes of the tax collector. Tax collectors were horrible, awful backstabbers. They had betrayed their people, and they understood their own betrayal. The tax collector's alms were not welcome at the Temple. They were outcasts of society, even though they had the power to tax you—and if you didn't pay, you'd find Roman soldiers at your house. When Jesus had dinner with a tax collector, it wasn't stuffy, religious legalists who got angry. It was *everyone*. Jesus was hanging out with traitors. And as an oppressed minority, the Judeans had no tolerance for traitors.

We would have felt the exact same way. We would have been angry at Jesus too. Proverbs 11:1 says that "a false balance is an abomination to the LORD, but an accurate weight is his delight." Scripture condemned their tax collecting. They were sinners of the worst kind.

Jesus invited them to join him.

Jesus was constantly with the wrong people.

Why was he talking to women?

To Samaritans?

To tax collectors?

Jesus never seemed to have a moral standard for the people who came around him. On occasion the gospels tell us he encouraged them to "sin no more," but he never kept them out because of their sin. On a regular basis, his disciples or the religious leaders were scandalized and offended by those Jesus welcomed into his presence. Children. Women. Prostitutes. Tax collectors. Romans. Lepers. Beggars. Samaritans. In fact, Jesus got the most angry at those most focused on sin: the religious leaders who would classify other people as "sinners."

Jesus ate with the wrong people.

He hung out with the wrong people.

He demonstrated through his life that there aren't wrong and right people.

There are just people.

5 The type of inclusion Jesus practiced gets you in trouble. This type of inclusion you just don't do. This type of inclusion gets you labeled as an outcast. This type of inclusion gets you killed.

It's not giving sight to the blind or raising people from the dead that is impressive about Jesus. It's his fellowship with society's worst outcasts—which automatically made *him* an outcast. That's miraculous.

Jesus saw Matthew and said to this traitorous outcast, this untouchable dirtbag, "Let's try to change the world."

6 The real church ought to be doing this.
We ought to be becoming outcasts by befriending outcasts.

We should be ridiculed for hanging out with the ridiculous.

We should be known for irrational grace. Irrational forgiveness.

That's more important than any miracle, any point of doctrine.

But I don't see this Jesus in the church today. This guy who hung out with the wrong people all of the time wouldn't write a discipline manual for his church, or design a system for how to kick a sinner out of his congregation. He'd be having a meal with them. He'd invite them to join him at his table, with prostitutes and cheats. (He'd also turn water into wine, which would get him kicked out of a good many evangelical churches.)

I wouldn't want Jesus in my church if he showed up today because of the people Jesus would hang out with. I would think, "I don't know how he can love them and love me too." They would piss me off, the kind of people Jesus would love. I would be thinking, "Why would Jesus hang out with such assholes?" He'd hang out with people like zealots, and I would think, "Where is Jesus's nonviolence?" He'd hang out with the one percent, and I would think, "Where is Jesus's love for the oppressed?"

I can't imagine accepting that Jesus if he showed up today. I'd argue for hours that some guy's theology is ruining people, and Jesus would show grace and remember that same guy's a husband and a father, he's got kids and a wife. Jesus would go to his house and have a meal with him. Jesus would stand on stage and say, "This guy's a real human being. A person, just like you and me."

7 Do we really love our enemies? And I don't mean will I love someone who gossiped about me. No. Will I love someone who killed someone close to me? Will I love someone who betrayed my family? Will I love someone who cheated on me?

That's Jesus's example. That example isn't what people see in the church. They see a bunch of people arguing about who is in and who is out.

Jesus says to everyone the church says is out:

Come on in.

Chapter 11

Hoping in the Unseen

I cannot be an optimist, but I am a prisoner of hope.

—Cornel West

1 I did a funeral down in Mississippi recently for a man named Red, my friend's father. It was my first Southern funeral in a long time—multiple viewings, an open casket at the service where I spoke, a graveside service in about a hundred and fifty degrees. Afterward, cold fried chicken and casserole.

My friend's parents had been together for fifty-eight years. Fifty-eight years is a long time. That's more than some people's entire lives. Red and Polly had been together for almost six decades.

Now Polly was alone.

I know aloneness, even if I don't know it in the same way Polly does. I lost my mom to cancer a few years ago. I can remember when I got the call telling me that she wasn't going to be here long. I wanted to come right away, but I waited until the morning to get on a flight. By the morning, I got another call: she was gone.

I went to the airport. I've got to be normal, I thought. Check in my luggage. Go through security. Sit and wait for the plane. Stand in line to board. Everything's got to be normal. I put on some Johnny Cash and tried to get myself into a zone where I didn't think about her. But it didn't work. I could remember, just months before, pushing her around in her wheelchair, trying to maneuver her and her oxygen machine around a Christmas antique show in Charlotte. I'd give anything just to relive the most mundane moments with her.

All I remember hearing about death as a kid was "If you died tonight, where would you go?" They never asked, "If you died tonight, how would your friends and family go on?"

2 Death is the reality everyone deals with, but it seems that nobody wants to talk about. My mom was the closest person I ever had, and then she was gone. People who called themselves my friends, who wouldn't hesitate to call me up or email me or argue with me publicly, were silent. They didn't know what to do.

I'm not sure I knew what to do with death either.

The idea of heaven didn't work for me when my mom died. I felt certain that she was in heaven, with God, and happier—all the things Christians normally believe—but all I could think about was never being able to see her, call her, talk to her, for the rest of my life.

We Christians have such certainty about the afterlife that we repress the deep sadness of knowing we will never see this person again, that we are going to go through the rest of our lives without this person. Often we don't fully embrace death for what it is; we gloss over it with talks of mansions and streets of gold.

Death is a tragedy. It's important to walk through that grief without being bombarded with assurances that everything is okay. Heaven doesn't deal with the fact that I can't see my mom now. I want to pick up the phone to call her and I can't. I'll be at a restaurant or a store and pick up a smell or a sound and it'll take me right back to Mom. Heaven doesn't deal with the fact that a perfume or a type of chocolate might have me in tears in public simply because I remember that she liked it.

Instead we say, "They're in a better place."

"We'll see them again someday."

"They're with the Lord now."

I don't find offense in those things, those happy clichés that are supposed to make you feel better. When you don't know what to say, clichés are the first things that come to your mind. I've done so many funerals where people are surprised by the loss and are in shock, and these words roll off our tongues without a thought. It's our way of saying, "Holy shit, I don't know what just happened."

On the other hand, we say those things so much that we start believing them. We think there's a reason for everything, that this is part of God's plan, or that God will turn it into something good.

Both Luke and John record Jesus countering the idea that sin causes suffering, which is what his disciples supposed. In Luke 13, Jesus's conclusion is that it could happen to any of us. In John 9, Jesus says that a man has been born blind so God's power could be shown through him—and then he heals the man. This isn't an explanation of human suffering, but an integral part of this one story, this singular event.

Jesus leaves us without a theology of suffering.

Once you've been through grief, you discover there's only one thing you can say: "There are no words." It's almost a code for those of us who have gone through loss. There are no words. The people who can say that to you know what it is like. They know that you can't express it; they've been there, and that's enough, knowing that someone's been there, that you're not traveling a road that no one's ever traveled.

I knew a family whose twenty-one-year-old was hit by a car. There was nothing to say to comfort them but "This is horrible and awful." It wasn't God's plan or God's opportunity to make something good. It was simply a tragedy.

It isn't in the denial of tragedy but the embrace of it that we find hope.

3 At the same time that my mom was dying, people confronted me in person, on the phone, or online, telling me "in love" what they thought of my position toward homosexuality, saying they loved me. None of them asked how my family was doing. No one asked me how I was handling my mom's illness. Their only concern was making sure I was set straight in the "truth" about gays and lesbians.

At the time, we had a sticker for the church in Atlanta that apologized on behalf of Christians for being self-righteous, arrogant bastards. We'd post them around the city. A pastor friend emailed me to say he loved me, but he felt our stickers were offensive and hurtful and wanted me to take them down. He said that the church had been bad-mouthed enough. He loved me, he said again. He was doing this out of love. And not a word about my mom.

I feel sorry for anyone who tried to argue with me about theology during that time. The experience gave me perspective. I didn't want theology to ever become more important than people. It made me realize that I never want to be clueless. I'm certain that Jesus discussed theology only when he saw people being rejected, when he saw people using their religion to justify prejudice and exclusion. That's when Jesus would pull out the big ideas.

★   ★   ★

At the end of Red's funeral, Polly was hugging every-body, and I thought to myself, Don't let her hug me. Please don't let her hug me. But she did, and I fell apart. I lost it.

Seeing Red's family deal with his death was a spiritual experience for me. I spend a lot of my time reading and talking about theology and philosophy and faith and doubt. But when I find myself in a place where people are remembering a life long lived and grieving their loss, I want to sit down and ask *them* what life's about. What really matters.

I tried to be as transparent as possible at Red's funeral, even though I knew it could backfire. "I know some say this is God's will, but then I'd say that God's will sucks." When your loved one is gone, it doesn't matter the reason, it doesn't matter what your faith is. It hurts. I tried to escape the pain. I went to a movie; and for an hour and a half I escaped. But the moment the credits rolled, the pain came back with such hid-eous force I decided I never wanted to escape it again.

4 Years after my mom died, I finally was able to grieve. And as I did, I found myself spending hours on the back porch of my friend Pete's house, chain smoking and having him deconstruct my theology. It was brutal; I felt alone, abandoned, hollow, and frustrated. I wasn't angry at God. But I did doubt that God even existed. Even a grace-filled, loving God seemed pretty impotent in those moments of grief. As I mourned my mother, I discovered the meaninglessness of life in those moments, my inability to deal with loss, and my refusal to deal with my own emotions. In those moments I embraced futility—and found hope.

There are many things I hope in. Heaven. Grace. God. I've come from a point of believing in them to hoping in them, because hope recognizes futility. It recognizes doubt.

At Red's funeral, I read from Romans.

> In hope that the creation itself will be set free from its bondage to decay, and will obtain the freedom of the glory of the children of God. We know that the whole creation has been groaning in labor pains until now. And not only the creation, but we ourselves, who have the first fruits of the Spirit, groan inwardly while we wait for adoption, the redemption of our bodies. For in hope we were saved. Now hope that is seen is not hope. For who hopes for what is seen? But if we hope for what we do not see, we wait for it with patience.[*]

"Hope that is seen is not hope," Paul says. Hope comes from a place of doubt. It comes from an inability to see. You don't hope for one plus one to equal

---

[*] Romans 8:20–25.

two. You hope for heaven. You hope for an afterlife. But because you haven't *seen* it, you also doubt. You wonder. You may be skeptical. But you hope.

Lately I have seen this hope in the Bible. In the Sermon on the Mount, Jesus says "Blessed are the poor"—that is, those who doubt they are going to have enough money to make it each day. "Blessed are the meek"—those who doubt themselves. "Blessed are those who mourn"—those who doubt that they can go on in the face of their suffering. Blessed are the doubters. Blessed are those that hope.

I'm naturally a pessimist. I hope things are going to turn out okay (but they're probably not). The only things you don't have to doubt are death and taxes.* That's where Jesus's words speak so deeply to me. Not that I can be certain that my mourning will be turned into laughter. Not that I can be certain that I will inherit the earth. But whatever those things mean, I can hope. I can still be a hopeful skeptic. Skepticism makes my hope stronger.

5 So many in the church are dealing with grief. It shakes our faith, causing us to doubt, and yet we can't talk to anyone who responds well to our doubt. So we put it off or hide it. As Christians,

---

* I got a letter from Atlanta that looked like a scam, but it turns out that in 1994 or something, I left off $800 from a tax return, and some collection agency had been sending letters to an old address and finally they found me. You *will* pay taxes.

we fall back on clichés to help ourselves forget our real emotions, or we go to therapists or take time off to deal with things, expecting everything to work out in time.

But we need to be there for one another. We need to allow doubt to be spoken to each other on a regular basis so when we go through tragedy and grief, we aren't caught unaware or uncomfortable with the mourning process. We need to give people permission to embrace death, tragedy, the meaninglessness of life.

The grieving person needs grace, and not just the first time, but over and over and over again. I've heard people say someone is "an emotional wreck" or "needy" or "clingy." These aren't words that love uses. Love doesn't expect a solution. Love doesn't need someone to "get better" to validate their patience and empathy. Love comes back again and again and again.

We need to embrace others' brokenness because before too long, we'll discover our own.

6 Grace for grieving people looks different for everyone. I don't have the answers, and I'm not sure there are answers on how to best help people grieve. Sometimes you need to grieve with them. Sometimes you need to do the simple things— bring them food, clean their house, repaint a room. If they want to talk, talk. If they don't, don't. If they're hungry, eat. If they're not, don't.

The most important thing a grieving person needs is grace.

A friend who worked at a church lost his father, and a month later he was fired. For that church, after about thirty days, you need to just "get over it."

Or consider the church whose pastor has been caught in a scandal. Most churches' first reaction is, "You've sinned, and we need to fix you." Or worse, "You've sinned, and we need to be rid of you." But this pastor has to grieve their own loss as well, and deal with the hurt and self-loathing of having hurt loved ones and lost the trust of the community. The hurt of betrayal causes people to lash out without grace.

Grace doesn't mean you can't still be hurt. But it does mean that you put yourself in the other person's shoes and discover without prejudice what it means to be on the other side of the situation.

7 Soon after my mom died, my wife left me. It hurt. I felt betrayed. I was angry. But I also tried to put myself in her shoes. I tried to make sure that our friends weren't taking sides. She'd just lost her marriage and her mother-in-law too. I wasn't necessarily very good at putting myself in her shoes, but I tried. It wasn't easy or clear-cut, and both of us needed healing and restoration.

Going through the breakup of a marriage makes me realize that not only is doubt a necessary part of hope, but it's also part of love. Even when you love someone so much that you think you'll love them forever, there's still that little doubt of "maybe they don't love me back" or "what if someone else comes along?"

At Red's funeral, I read more of Romans, and I think it's meaningful here.

> For I am convinced that neither death, nor life, nor angels, nor rulers, nor things present, nor things to come, nor powers, nor height, nor depth, nor anything else in all creation, will be able to separate us from the love of God in Christ Jesus our Lord. I am speaking the truth in Christ—I am not lying; my conscience confirms it by the Holy Spirit.*

I imagine Paul dictating this letter and getting a little carried away. It's almost like he has a flash of inspiration and shouts like a Pentecostal preacher: "Nothing will separate us, I'm sure of it, the Holy Spirit tells me so!" This moment takes all doubt and insecurity away for Paul—Paul, who told us that the greatest of all these is love.

Paul told us that love hopes all things. Love endures all things.

There's doubt in there—hoping for all things—but also faithfulness when hope is gone. There's hope for that which is unseen, unknown—but also endurance when it all falls apart. That's God's love, not always love here on earth among people.

---

* Romans 8:38–9:1.

In marriage, there were things that I hoped I could love through, but I couldn't. I was too hurt and torn apart. It's hard when you realize that even your love is not perfect. You hope it would be, but it doesn't always work that way. It isn't always unconditional. When Paul says nothing will separate us from the love of God, we realize that the only perfect love is outside of being. It's outside of matter. It's outside of our understanding. We can only hope and have faith that it's really there.

8 I hoped that God would heal my mom, but she died. I hoped that my marriage would stay together, but it didn't. But I still hope that other people will be healed, will make it through the tough times.

Hopelessness is being so far beyond doubt that you've given up. But that doesn't mean that hope is without doubt. We can't conquer hopelessness with certainty. We can only embrace the doubt in hope. We can only be a prisoner of hope.

Chapter 12

Losing Belief, Finding Faith

Hoping against hope. —Romans 4:18

1 After I saw the movie *The Hunger Games*, a libertarian friend sent me an email telling me the movie supports the libertarian point of view. I emailed back and said, "No, I don't think it's that at all," and explained how it fit my political ideals. The next morning I saw an article online saying something like "every political party thinks *The Hunger Games* is about them."

What's going on in our country, in politics, is the same thing going on in the church today: a lack of real dialogue, with pundits proclaiming what their hearers already know. It all boils down to this idea of *absolute truth*. No matter what you believe, when you hold that belief as absolutely true, when you are certain of its truth, you lose your dignity. People wonder why Christians can be such asses, but when we claim to have absolute truth, there's no *conversation with*, there's only *preaching at*. When we believe that the result of being wrong is hellfire and damnation, we lose any reason to consider conversation as beneficial. It even twists our idea of love to where we think love is expressed in our closed-mindedness. It twists our idea of justice to where we think justice is the damnation that results from someone's rejection of our absolute truth.

It's like that scene in *Saved!* "I am *filled* with Christ's love!" we say, and throw a Bible at someone's face because we are so certain we have a corner on the truth.

2 I can see the appeal of certainty, though. Certainty promises that things will never change. It promises that you'll never have to rethink things or be confronted with a reality that you can't understand. It offers a sense of safety from the unfamiliar or foreign.

But certainty, far from being safe, can bring about a kind of death. Jesus said these words to the Pharisees of his day: "For you are like whitewashed tombs, which on the outside look beautiful, but inside they are full of the bones of the dead and all kinds of filth."* You look great on the outside, but inside you're miserable and dying.

My life has been a story of coming to grips with uncertainty. Certainty can make us mean and messy and hateful. Certainty allows God to become our alibi for hate and judgment. Certainty helps us cover up our brokenness and our fears.

Certainty is also divisive. Some people believe in free will, while others believe in predestination. Some people believe in speaking in tongues, while others believe that speaking in tongues is just a bunch of babbling. Some believe that God is an idea, while others think that God is a male spiritual being who looks down from heaven. Still others think God is midichlorians. Denominations spin off denominations, and the spinoff denominations spin off more denominations, because everyone wants a church where everyone agrees with them on each point, enjoys the same kind of service, and rallies around the same cause.

A pastor's wife once told me that if I don't believe in a literal Adam and Eve, then my faith falls apart. If you're not certain about everything, then you can't be certain about anything.† That's a dangerous idea, that all or nothing.

---

* Matthew 23:27.

† Someone else asked me, "Do you believe all the stories in the Bible are true?" How are you supposed to respond to that? I guess you say no, but then they say, "Ah, so you don't believe that it's the Word of God," and then you're like, well, it's impossible to get out full ideas on Twitter. Damn you, Twitter.

But Jesus didn't do all or nothing. He summed up the law and the prophets. He stopped reading in the middle of Isaiah. He said whatever you bind on earth will be bound in heaven. He said you will do even greater things than these.

3 Certainty also requires a source, so people say they have it figured all out through the Bible. But many who've figured it out based on the Bible don't understand why the Bible was written, to whom it was written, or the history of the times when it was written. They just take it at face value and say it's obvious, it's right here in black and white. Context, to them, means nothing.

The other day I was trying to explain to someone why I'm open and affirming of LGBTQ people, and I recommended a book about the issue. The person balked. "Why should I have to read a whole book about the subject? Just point me to the verse in the Bible that says it's okay." There's no arguing there. You're going to find that in the modern English translations of the Bible from the end of the last century, you're not going to get an "it's okay to be gay" any more than you'll find a verse saying that war, slavery, abortion, or interracial marriage is wrong or right. In fact, if we were to take everything written in two-thousand-year-old manuscripts as black and white, we'd do a lot of strange things.

And so apologetics was born. Growing up, I

thought apologetics was apologizing for everything that the Bible said. ("I'm sorry that the Bible says you're going to hell.") It turned out to be worse: trying to prove that everything the Bible says is right, or using the Bible to prove that a certain theology is better than another. It's convincing someone else that you are right, which is just a nice way of saying that they are wrong. They take a collection of books—the Bible—and claim to have everything figured out. They might not understand everything it says, but eventually they assume they will. They've turned the Bible into a law book, a constitution. Theologians and pastors become lawyers, arguing nuances and loopholes that the original writers would never have imagined. They act as if God can be figured out if you just study the Bible enough.

4   What's funny is that the God of the "certain" often starts to look pretty American. Things that are "biblical" start to closely resemble our own cultural values. God loves the people we love and despises the people we despise. We build a structure and confuse the structure with God; so if there are ever any cracks in the structure we have to cover them up quickly, because otherwise it is our view of God who is cracking. We make people sign contracts and pledge money and affirm doctrines in order to be in community with us. We build an empire around our beliefs. We become the institution. Robert Holloway

warns that "the main law of institutional survival is that the many take precedence over the few. If institutions are to endure, they have to place higher value on their own endurance than their loyalty to individuals, no matter how attractive or charismatic they may be."[*] We have churches who are afraid of people, because the individual threatens the institution's existence. In this world, the lost sheep and lost coin remain lost, the man on the side of the road dies because no one will help him, and the prodigal son becomes a hired hand at best.

We accept that we have to love our neighbor, but we can still make war against our enemies and hate the gays for ruining the country. We come up with a kind of certainty that keeps us from having to deal with people who have different perspectives. We take God out of the everyday, out of the world, and put God in a museum. We decide that we are the keepers of God. And then we bestow upon this God all of our fears and repressed emotions and somehow allow God to justify those things in our minds. As we do so, this God begins to look less like love. God starts to love fewer and fewer people.

5 A God who loves everyone is a dangerous God. A God who loves *us* specifically is much more palatable. A God who is American, even more

---

[*] Holloway, *Doubts and Loves,* chapter 11.

LOSING BELIEF, FINDING FAITH

so, and a God who is *Americana*, with strong white men and submissive women? That *sells*. There's a cultural resurgence of Americana, 1950s ideals, and stereotypical masculinity, so it's attractive to think that God supports that as well. Man-pastors preach the manly God—you know, the God who expects men to hunt and fish and climb rocks and watch football and sweep long-skirted, flowing-haired swooning women off of their feet. The church loves these stereotypes.*

That's the kind of culture that I grew up in. The fat boy who couldn't do sports and got picked last for games got made fun of. This culture assumes men are breadwinners and sports lovers, and women are mothers, not leaders or teachers. It plays to stereotypes and popular opinion. If you preach those ideals, you're going to find success. And if you're already a chauvinist, why not join a chauvinist religion with a chauvinist God?

If you tell me that the Bible says to embrace my masculinity and have sex with my wife five days a week instead of talking about our emotions, sure, that's going to be attractive for a while. But eventually sex is just sex, and you're going to have to make conversation, not love.

When it comes to gender roles, the church has become irrelevant because we are practicing a selective version of two-thousand-year-old cultural ideas.

---

* And to someone like me, who likes music and comic books and decorating my house and painting Hot Wheels into Batmobiles and dressing manly—if by manly you mean like an extra from *The Wild One*—it's insulting.

Context is important for reading the Bible. The patriarchal, masculine language of the Bible is to be expected, considering the culture it was written in. In biblical societies, women were property.

But what Jesus and Paul were saying was countercultural and radical. When Jesus held theological discussions with women, when he praised Mary for sitting at his feet like a disciple, when he ate with tax collectors and prostitutes—that's interesting. So the patriarchal view of women in the church today isn't biblical; it's first-century Middle Eastern. Or even more ancient. Or backward, if you will.

6 Certainty isn't faith. We ought to use the phrase "losing your faith" to mean "gaining belief." Faith is not belief. Belief wants to have certainty, and so it puts faith aside. But faith is an affirmation of something that hasn't been seen, that can't be grasped. It's not certainty. If you're certain about something, you don't need faith. When you believe in something, you think you're right about it. When you have faith in something, you're open to the idea that you might be wrong.

Many in the church have lost their faith and traded it for certainty. In the process, they have lost God.

When you lose faith and find certainty, you close yourself off to the mystery of God. You limit God. You make God into your own image, and God ends up stuck in your space, your time, your culture, and your ideas and thoughts, which are based on your own natural prejudices and blind spots. You invent God.

The Buddhists have a saying that as soon as you think you've understood the Buddha, you have to kill the Buddha. If you think you are certain about what or who God is, then God is no bigger or greater than your limitations. Paul Tillich says when we can conceive God, God ceases to be God; "it is as atheistic to affirm the existence of God as it is to deny it."* God, to Tillich, is not a being, but being itself.

Certainty creates a God from my lenses, my ideas, and my thoughts. That's why we have to let go of certainty. With God you don't get certainty. We avoid God by embracing certainty. The Bible is filled with stories of avoiding God. Send Moses up the mountain to talk to God. Give us a king to rule us. Give us laws and practices and beliefs that we can use. Build us a temple for God to dwell within. Put God behind this curtain so only on certain days can certain people access God.

Then we'll know who is in and who is out: by who follows the rules, who does the right practices, and who believes the right things.

But scripture also contains a thread of wrong people being made right. Melchizedek. Rahab. Ruth. Adulterers. Lepers. Tax collectors. Samaritans. Gentiles. Romans. Eunuchs.

All accepted.

---

* Paul Tillich, *Systematic Theology,* 237.

All welcomed.

With God, you don't know who's in and who's out.

With God, you don't get certainty.

7 What should we do with all this uncertainty and doubt? The risk of faith is exposure to the unknown. No one wants the unknown. We want to know. We want to be certain. We want a *foundation*, something to hang on to, because life is messy. Life is tough.

Faith is like grace. It takes responsibility, not rules. It offers freedom, not security. But it is the way Jesus offers. It is the freedom from the law, and the responsibility to love.

Hold on to your truth, faith says, but your truth doesn't have to hold on to you. The freedom to have faith instead of belief is, to me, one of the most beautiful things about following Christ.

8 Faith doesn't deny that life is meaningless. It also doesn't accept that life is meaningless. Faith is living against meaninglessness.

I haven't got it figured out. But I've decided to live as if life has meaning. I'm going to live as though perhaps Jesus was the son of God. I'm going to live in the idea of grace. I'm going to love my neighbor as myself. I'm going to work to free people from hell on earth. I'm going to try to put food in the mouths of people who are hungry. I'm going to try to help end suffering for victims of the sex trade industry. I'm going to work to end genocide in Darfur. Even if life is meaningless, I'm going to work to end suffering.

How do you answer tragedy? Can there ever be an answer? When I was going through my mom's death and my divorce and the grieving process years later, I saw that most people answer tragedy with either "there is no God" or "God has a plan for good."* What kept me going was the discovery that I can embrace the world as good and meaningful even if it truly isn't—as though by embracing it as good, I just might make it so.

Paul says in Romans about Abraham: "Hoping against hope, he believed that he would become 'the father of many nations,' according to what was said."† This is faith—hoping against hope.

Hoping against hope that life has meaning.

9 I've found peace thinking that faith is bigger than I used to allow it to be. I've found peace in the mystery, peace as the black and white fade into gray. When I accept this mystery of faith, suddenly I don't have to worry about the rules. I don't have to worry about following them, and I don't have

---

* Or hardcore determinists like John Piper who conclude that tragedy is God's wrath upon everyone for sin.

† Romans 4:18.

to worry about who else is following them. I don't have to try to figure out who is in and who is out. I don't have to separate myself from God. I don't need to hide behind rules and practices and beliefs in order to convince myself that somehow I'm safe. I am comfortable with the risk of faith.

I find God as much in the small, dark coffee shop where I like to drink iced tea all day as I do in the church with incense and bells. I'm not knocking theologies and traditions, but rather the temptation to trust them too much, to hide our other Gods behind those traditions and avoid the true mystery of faith. We end up with our liberal Gods and conservative Gods as we insulate ourselves from the possibility that we are wrong, that we don't have it all figured out. We insulate ourselves from true transformation.

If God can be contained in someone's theology, in a book, in an interpretation of the Bible or a church's creed, then God is not very big. If God is love, and love is contained within these ancient books, then love isn't that great. We try to defend this God who loves us and will torture us if we don't love back; a God who promises streets of gold if you do the right thing and hellfire if you don't. I can't do that anymore.

Instead, I want to be in love. Not in love with Jesus, like the God-is-my-girlfriend worship songs. But when you're in love, life has meaning. You can't help but feel everything has meaning when you're in love. Love compels you to see meaning in everything and hope even against hope. You think, I can't wait to see this person. You think about them every day, and when you aren't with them, time moves slowly. When you are with them, it seems like you never have enough time. When you're in love, everything else fades. Instead of complaining, you find yourself daydreaming. Instead of worrying, you are planning your next date.

And there's nothing you can do to make yourself fall in love; it just clicks.

But being in love has its risks. It can cause heartbreak. When you're heartbroken, no matter what you believe about the world, life feels hopeless. Meaningless. Hollow. Your hurt is overwhelming. None of your friends know what to say; no magic words will heal the hurt. You think life is just hell. You hope against hope that you'll find that kind of love again.

Isn't love worth the risk?

Isn't it worth finding an uncontrollable love, beyond doubt or reason or reality or meaninglessness, a love that hopes against hope that life can be meaningful and beautiful?

Conclusion

Unconditionally

At some thoughts a man stands perplexed, above all at the sight of human sin, and he wonders whether to combat it by force or by humble love. Always decide: "I will combat it by humble love." If you resolve on that once for all, you can conquer the whole world.

—*Fyodor Dostoyevsky,* The Brothers Karamazov

In Luke chapter 10 we read this story about Jesus:

Now as they went on their way, he entered a certain village, where a woman named Martha received him into her home. She had a sister named Mary, who sat at the Lord's feet and listened to what he was saying. But Martha was distracted by her many tasks; so she came to him and asked, "Lord, do you not care that my sister has left me to do all the work by myself? Tell her then to help me." But the Lord answered her, "Martha, Martha, you are worried and distracted about many things; there is need of only one thing. Mary has chosen the better part, which will not be taken away from her."*

Jesus says Martha is worried and distracted about many things. I know what it is like to be worried about and distracted by many things. One of my first worries was about the eternal destination of my soul. On several occasions as a kid, I bluntly told my dad, "Dad, the only reason I don't kill myself is because I don't want to go to hell." His response was always, "Son, that's kept me from taking my own life a few times as well."

As I've already said, I used to be very concerned about the Bible as an inerrant text because I had been taught that if you tossed out any part of the Bible, all the truths of scripture would come tumbling down like the walls of Jericho. I had to prove the Bible was true. I had to defend the Bible against attackers.

Now, I find myself concerned with the people I love—my sister, my friends. But Tillich writes, "Nothing by which its very nature is finite can rightly become a matter of ultimate concern." He goes on:

Many boys are ruined because they make their mother their ultimate concern. The mother cannot help but be a very high symbol of concern,

---

* Luke 10:38–42.

but the moment she is made a matter of ultimate concern—or deified (it is always unconscious, of course)—the consequences are always destructive. So if we make a finite reality into God, we enter the realm of idolatry...the consequences are always destructive.*

This is one of the reasons some leave the faith after the Bible is shown to be finite—because we've elevated it to infinite. We've committed idolatry with the Bible. The Bible is finite, meaning it has *limits*, limits of language, culture, and authorship.

I experienced this idolatry firsthand with my father. He was imprisoned for five years, and I fought for most of those years to get him freed. While he was in prison, I viewed him as a hero who could do nothing wrong. When he got out of prison, our relationship fell apart almost immediately. We were together a month and couldn't stand each other. I expected my father to be this infinite, ultimate hero, when instead he is a finite, fallible human being—a person with limits. I've done this many times with people in my life, with authors and speakers and friends, and it always ends badly. In every area of my life, the consequence of deep concern—my concern about the eternal consequences of my actions, my concern with defending the Bible, my concern for my father—was destructive.

---

* D. Mackenzie Brown, "Ultimate Concern—Tillich in Dialogue," accessed July 2012, http://www.religion-online.org/showchapter.asp?title=538&C=599.

Jesus tells Martha that though she is worried and distracted by many things, only one thing matters. What is this one thing? Tillich hesitates to give an answer for that one concern Mary has chosen. And I understand why. Is it religion? No; we have no reason to believe Martha was any less religious than Mary, and religion, as beliefs and activities, is a finite concern. It's not God, for as Tillich says, "God can be made a finite concern, an object among other objects; in whose existence some people believe and some do not. Such a God, of course, cannot be our ultimate concern. Or we make him a person like other persons with whom it is useful to have a relationship."*

Tillich decides that Mary is concerned "ultimately, unconditionally, infinitely." Her *infinite concern* is the "one thing" Jesus speaks of "that will not be taken away from her." Tillich says that by being concerned unconditionally and infinitely, "we look at our finite concerns...[and] everything seems the same and yet everything is changed. We are still concerned about all these things but differently—the anxiety is gone! It still exists and tries to return. But its power is broken; it cannot destroy us any more."†

What was Jesus's concern? When Jesus gets intense and a little crazy, talking about millstones tied around necks, he's coming to the defense of children and the oppressed. When Jesus talks about eternity, infinite,

---

* Tillich, *The New Being,* chapter 20.

† Tillich, *The New Being,* chapter 20.

unconditional things, however, it is within the context of love: with all your heart, with all your soul, with all your mind, with all your strength.

Tillich says, "We see the unconditional ultimate should not be viewed as part of a pyramid even if it's placed at the top, for the ultimate is that which is the ground and the top at the same time.... It is that which embraces everything."*

Love is that which embraces everything. It is that to which I can give myself ultimately, unconditionally. By dying with Christ and rising with him, I can be grasped by ultimate, unconditional concern. My sister is not my ultimate concern, but I can give myself to loving her unconditionally. My friends are not my ultimate concern, but I can give myself to loving them infinitely. In fact, Jesus tells me that my enemies are not my ultimate concern, but that I might take the risk to love them ultimately, unconditionally, infinitely.

I am no longer concerned with an afterlife, though I am concerned with eternity. I am no longer concerned with inerrancy, though I am concerned with the beautiful mess that is the Bible. I am no longer concerned with eliminating doubt—my faith has become the life partner of my doubt, and I love how cute they are together. Love has transformed and will continue to transform the way I am concerned about, interact with, and respond to everything.

---

* Tillich, *The New Being,* chapter 20.

Writer's Note

One of the first things Jay Bakker ever said to me in person was "Are you the devil?" I was taken aback at this turn in the conversation, especially since it presupposed the existence of Satan. We hadn't even established theological common ground yet. But it turns out that my cup of coffee was so hot that he could barely see my face through the steam, and I was sipping away at it nonetheless. Naturally he figured only a creature of pure evil could stand such a hot beverage.

We lasted in Brooklyn only an hour or so before we headed out to the suburbs to a friend's house to spend a few days working on this book. First order of business, however, was for Jay to show me exactly how far he had gotten through *Batman: Arkham City* on the PS3, because I had yet to pick up my own copy of the game. Jay and I aren't that far apart in age, but far enough that he still had his PlayStation hooked to his TV through RCA cables. Far enough, actually, that he hadn't grown up with video games quite like I had. For me, the ×, ○, □, and △ are second nature, but for Jay, it's the fact that it's Batman that had him playing video games, and he had a tendency to accidentally shoot the Batarang out every few seconds. He couldn't believe how fast I could play. And once I hooked up the HDMI cables, he couldn't believe how much more awesome Batman looks in HD.

So before we ever wrote a word of this book, we defeated Mr. Freeze at least once.

Actually, one of the very first things Jay ever told me on the phone was that I was going to need a pseudonym to write with him. I assumed he didn't like my name for some reason, like it would be too long on the cover of the book. My dad jokingly went by the surname "Smith" in college because everyone had trouble with Meisenheimer, so I wasn't all that surprised. But Jay was just worried that my career in Christian publishing would tank after I became associated with him. He needn't have worried.

When it was time for me to fly home, Jay and Pete, whom we'd been staying with, stuck me on the train into Grand Central Station and said "good luck." I'd never been to New York, and once I found myself in the taxi line at Grand Central with only two hours until my flight, I might have panicked a little. I called Pete, and he told me to walk a block and hail a cab. I said, "How the hell do I do that?" He told me to put my hand in the air.

Eventually a cabbie pulled up; I hopped in and we

took off. I told him I loved New York, and he told me about the strict transportation authority. He asked what I do, and I told him I work with books. First he asked if I had any that I could give him, but when I said no, he asked me what kind of books. I told him books trying to help people live better. A gross over-simplification, but I hope it's true.

After a few minutes of silence, he asks me in his heavy accent, "If someone have no good job, what you say to them?"

At first I didn't know what he was really asking. If someone doesn't like their job? If someone doesn't have a job? I wasn't really sure. I fumbled my way through something about finding meaning in rela-tionships, loving people, choices—it was kind of a mess.

I called Mandy and told her I had no idea how far away I was from the airport, but I was hoping to get home on time anyway. The cabbie and I didn't speak for a while, and I fell to watching the clock tick away the precious minutes before my flight.

Then, at a stoplight, I catch my driver writing some-thing on a sheet of paper. He says the words aloud as he writes "If—someone—have—no—good—job—then..." and he hands me the paper and the pencil. "Here," he says.

I look at the paper and think, What would Jay say?

In big block letters, I write LOVE. And hand it back to him.

"Love?" he says. "Love? Jesus?"

"Sure," I say. "Jesus. Gandhi. Martin Luther King Jr." I feel like Jay would say this, too, but I can only guess.

We go back to a comfortable silence, but later, at another stoplight, I see him holding the sheet of paper on his leg, looking down at my pencil-scrawled advice. Love is not a very practical answer, but perhaps it might provoke good questions.

I tipped the guy well, made my flight, and arrived home in time to see my kids before bed.

A few weeks later, Jay came to Michigan and spent a weekend with Mandy and me, enjoying fine local cuisine and the affections of our dogs, who lay at his feet as if he were some sort of ancient rabbi. We talked nonstop about faith, Pentecostals, Pete Rollins, and PTL. We said weird things like "powered by pancakes" that probably only I found funny. We didn't play any video games; this was serious business now.

And now you're reading this book. You might not care too much about whose name is hiding underneath Jay's on the cover. But for Mandy and me, we're excited to be a part of what Jay's doing with this book and with Revolution NYC. No pseudonyms needed. This is good stuff.

Acknowledgments

Jay Bakker thanks:

My sweet girl, Karin Aebersold.

To those directly involved in the book: Andy Meisenheimer, Mandy Meisenheimer, Jim Kast-Keat, Wendy Grisham, Adrienne Ingrum, Chris and Anne Ammons, David Brokaw, and Brian and Jill Olson.

Also: Pete Rollins, Reverend Vince Anderson, Karal Hand, Bart Campolo, Tony Jones, Brian McLaren, Brennan Manning, Paul Tillich, Paolo Mello, Phil Harrison, Richard Holloway, Don Lemon, James and Jonathan Chapman, Daina Martin, Alfred Pennyworth, Randy and Gary Eddy-McCain, Ryan Downey, Dr. Jack Drescher, Bo and Shannon Julian, PFLAG, Pete's Candy Store, and Mom and Dad.

And also all of you reading this book, those of you who come to Revolution NYC, those of you who find me at conferences and sit down and chat with me—thank you. Whether you know it or not, you've been there with me in the past, and I hope you'll be there with me in the future. Between us, this can be a place of transparency, a place where worries and doubts and hurts and pains are welcome. A place where we choose love over our differences and community over certainty. Because whether you are an atheist or a saint, you are a part of a family; brothers and sisters. Family is family, and whether you're sharing uncomfortable moments or growing through conflict, you never leave your family.

Andy Meisenheimer thanks:

Jay, for allowing me to try to capture his voice on paper.

Wendy, for her guidance and support.

Adrienne, for encouraging me as a writer.

Pete, for putting in a good word for me.

Lyn, for starting me on this journey.

Jim, for friendship, enthusiasm, and beer.

My kids; they're the best part of my life.

And Mandy—my favorite critic, cowriter, and conversation partner.

It's not really my book, but I appreciate this chance to express my gratitude.

About the Authors

JAY BAKKER is co-pastor of Revolution NYC, a gay rights activist, and the winner of the 2012 PFLAG Straight for Equality in Faith Communities award. He is a grace enthusiast, a dyslexic, introverted pessimist, and a prisoner of hope. He lives in Brooklyn, New York.

www.revolutionnyc.com

ANDY MEISENHEIMER is a writer, editor, and stay-at-home dad. He and his family live in Manhattan, New York.